maranGraphics' ™
Simplified User Guide for Microsoft ®
MS-DOS® 5.0

Richard Maran

maranGraphics Inc.
Mississauga, Ontario, Canada

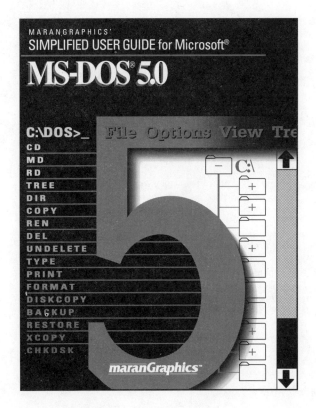

maranGraphics' ™
Simplified User Guide for Microsoft ®
MS-DOS™ 5.0

Copyright ©   maranGraphics Inc. 1991
5755 Coopers Avenue
Mississauga, Ontario
Canada
L4Z 1R9
(416) 890-3300

Screen Shots © 1981-1991 Microsoft
Corporation. Reprinted with permission
from Microsoft Corporation.

Published 1991.

Canadian Cataloguing in Publication Data

Maran, Richard
    MaranGraphics' simplified user guide for
Microsoft MS-DOS 5.0

Includes index.
ISBN 0-9694290-4-5

1. MS-DOS (Computer operating system).
I. Title.

QA76.76.O63M3 1991   005.4'46   C91-094651-5

Wholesale distribution:
Firefly Books Ltd.
250 Sparks Avenue
Willowdale, Ontario
Canada
M2H 2S4

Acknowledgements

Special thanks to Allan Fulcher, Mike Hedley and
Chris McKernan of Microsoft Canada Inc., and Ruth
Maran of maranGraphics for their support and
consultation.

To the dedicated staff at maranGraphics Inc. and
HyperImage Inc., including Monica DeVries, Lynne
Hoppen, Jim C. Leung, Robert Maran, and Elizabeth
Seeto for their artistic contribution.

To Eric Feistmantl who was always there to solve my
technical and operational problems.

And finally to Maxine Maran for providing the
organizational skill to keep the project under control.

Trademark Acknowledgements

Cover Design:
Erich Volk

Art Direction:
Jim C. Leung

Production:
Monica DeVries
Jim C. Leung

Linotronic L-300 Output:
HyperImage Inc.

Table of Contents

USING THIS GUIDE

This Simplified User Guide displays —on each page— exactly what you see on the screen as you move through the MS-DOS 5.0 operating system.

1 Finding the Section and Chapter

While flipping through the pages of the guide, scan the right hand side of the page to locate the section and chapter you want.

2 Finding the Topic within the Chapter

Once you are within the desired chapter, scan the top right hand side of the page to locate the topic you want. Flip to that highlighted page.

COPY OR MOVE FILES

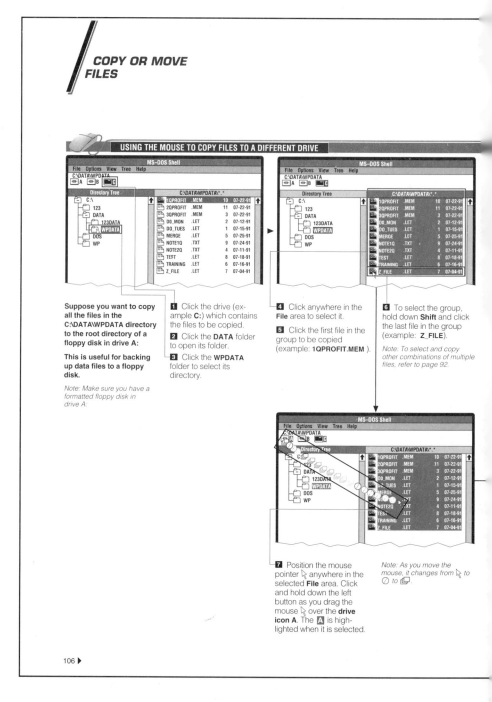

USING THE MOUSE TO COPY FILES TO A DIFFERENT DRIVE

Suppose you want to copy all the files in the C:\DATA\WPDATA directory to the root directory of a floppy disk in drive A:

This is useful for backing up data files to a floppy disk.

Note: Make sure you have a formatted floppy disk in drive A:

1 Click the drive (example **C:**) which contains the files to be copied.

2 Click the **DATA** folder to open its folder.

3 Click the **WPDATA** folder to select its directory.

4 Click anywhere in the **File** area to select it.

5 Click the first file in the group to be copied (example: **1QPROFIT.MEM**).

6 To select the group, hold down **Shift** and click the last file in the group (example: **Z_FILE**).

Note: To select and copy other combinations of multiple files, refer to page 92.

7 Position the mouse pointer ⏷ anywhere in the selected **File** area. Click and hold down the left button as you drag the mouse ⏷ over the **drive icon A**. The **A** is highlighted when it is selected.

Note: As you move the mouse, it changes from ⏷ to ⊘ to 🗀.

Using this Guide

Introduction to MS-DOS 5.0

Change Date or Time

Specify Drives and Directories

Internal and External Commands

Help

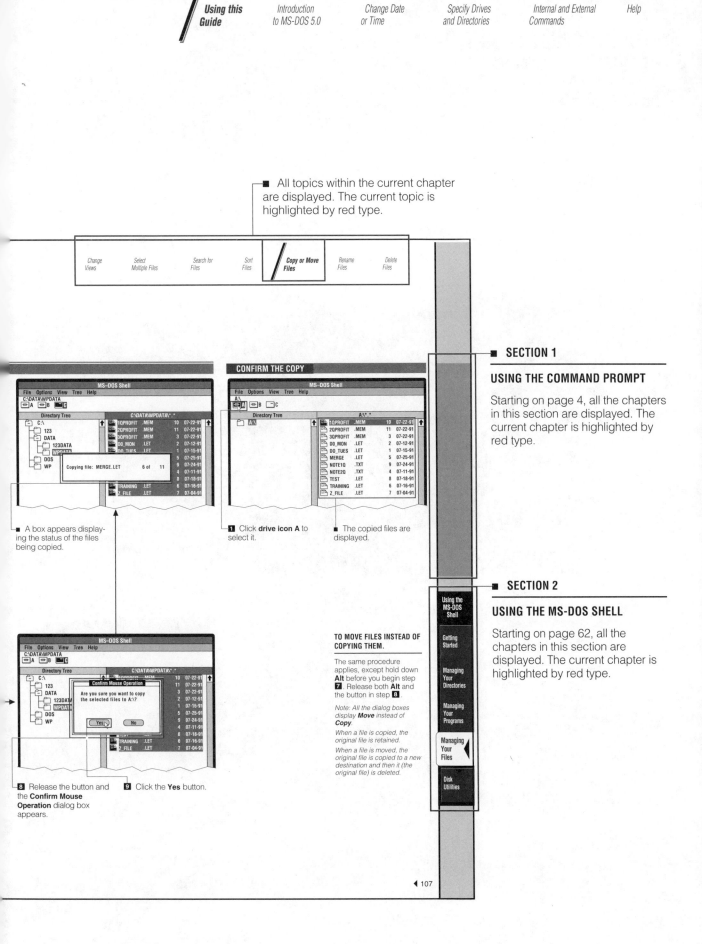

■ All topics within the current chapter are displayed. The current topic is highlighted by red type.

| Change Views | Select Multiple Files | Search for Files | Sort Files | **Copy or Move Files** | Rename Files | Delete Files |

Using the Command Prompt

Getting Started

Managing Your Directories

Managing Your Files

Managing Your Floppy Disks

Managing Your Hard Disk

■ **SECTION 1**

USING THE COMMAND PROMPT

Starting on page 4, all the chapters in this section are displayed. The current chapter is highlighted by red type.

CONFIRM THE COPY

Copying file: MERGE.LET   6 of 11

■ A box appears displaying the status of the files being copied.

1 Click **drive icon A** to select it.

■ The copied files are displayed.

■ **SECTION 2**

USING THE MS-DOS SHELL

Starting on page 62, all the chapters in this section are displayed. The current chapter is highlighted by red type.

Using the MS-DOS Shell

Getting Started

Managing Your Directories

Managing Your Programs

Managing Your Files

Disk Utilities

TO MOVE FILES INSTEAD OF COPYING THEM.

The same procedure applies, except hold down **Alt** before you begin step **7**. Release both **Alt** and the button in step **8**.

Note: All the dialog boxes display **Move** *instead of* **Copy**.

When a file is copied, the original file is retained.

When a file is moved, the original file is copied to a new destination and then it (the original file) is deleted.

Confirm Mouse Operation

Are you sure you want to copy the selected files to A:\?

Yes   No

8 Release the button and the **Confirm Mouse Operation** dialog box appears.

9 Click the **Yes** button.

◀ 107

◀ 3

1 Turn on the computer. It proceeds to do a diagnostic check on itself. If the check is OK, the computer beeps and within seconds the command prompt **C>** appears.

Note: Make sure you do not have a floppy disk in drive A: If you do, the computer will try to start MS-DOS from floppy drive A: instead of the hard drive.

ASSUMPTION

■ This guide assumes MS-DOS 5.0 is installed on your hard drive, in a subdirectory named \DOS.

■ To install MS-DOS 5.0, refer to your Microsoft User's Guide.

Note: If the MS-DOS Shell appears, press **F3** to return to the command prompt **C>**.

EXAMPLES

■ The examples in the guide are based on an IBM or compatible computer with a hard drive (C:) and two floppy drives (A: and B:).

■ All screen displays are based on MS-DOS Version 5.0.

Using this
Guide

*Introduction
to MS-DOS 5.0*

Change Date
or Time

Specify Drives
and Directories

Internal and External
Commands

Help

**Using the
Command
Prompt**

**Getting
Started**

Managing
Your
Directories

Managing
Your
Files

Managing
Your
Floppy Disks

Managing
Your
Hard Disk

The Microsoft Disk Operating System, or MS-DOS, is the most important program on your computer. It allows you to control and manage how the computer hardware and software work together.

MS-DOS could be described as a computer's central nervous system, or as traffic manager that keeps everything flowing smoothly.

MS-DOS is a collection of commands that allows the computer to:

- Receive instructions from you

- Work with application programs

- Manage application and data files

- Control and send information to the screen and peripheral devices (example: printers, modems, etc.)

THE MS-DOS SHELL – A GRAPHIC WAY TO WORK WITH MS-DOS

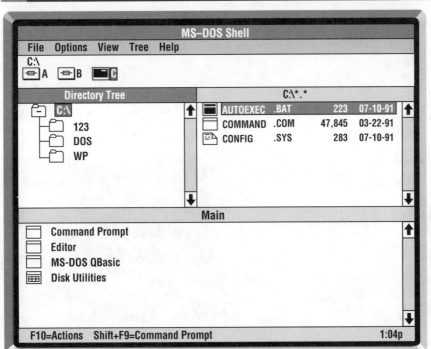

During the MS-DOS installation, you were asked if you wanted to run the MS-DOS Shell on startup.

If you chose Yes, the screen above appears.

The MS-DOS Shell is a visual interface that allows you to work more intuitively with the computer. It is described in detail starting on page 62.

To return to the command prompt **C>** from the MS-DOS Shell, press **F3**.

CHANGE DATE OR TIME

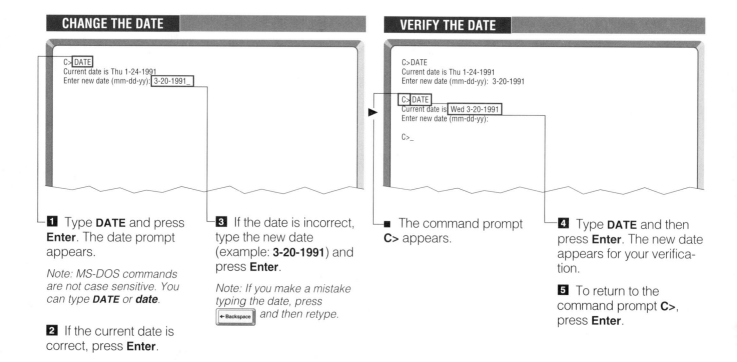

CHANGE THE DATE

```
C> DATE
Current date is Thu 1-24-1991
Enter new date (mm-dd-yy): 3-20-1991_
```

1 Type **DATE** and press **Enter**. The date prompt appears.

*Note: MS-DOS commands are not case sensitive. You can type **DATE** or **date**.*

2 If the current date is correct, press **Enter**.

3 If the date is incorrect, type the new date (example: **3-20-1991**) and press **Enter**.

Note: If you make a mistake typing the date, press `← Backspace` *and then retype.*

VERIFY THE DATE

```
C>DATE
Current date is Thu 1-24-1991
Enter new date (mm-dd-yy):  3-20-1991

C> DATE
Current date is Wed 3-20-1991
Enter new date (mm-dd-yy):

C>_
```

▪ The command prompt **C>** appears.

4 Type **DATE** and then press **Enter**. The new date appears for your verification.

5 To return to the command prompt **C>**, press **Enter**.

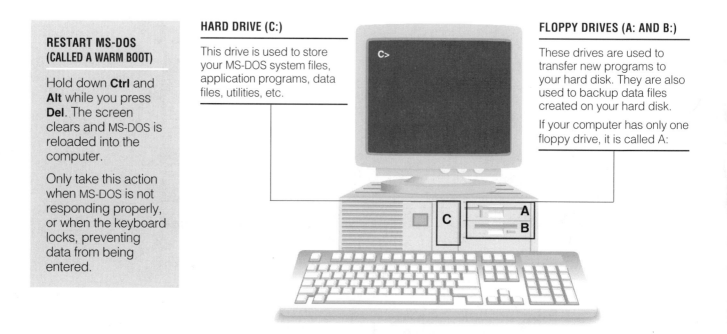

RESTART MS-DOS (CALLED A WARM BOOT)

Hold down **Ctrl** and **Alt** while you press **Del**. The screen clears and MS-DOS is reloaded into the computer.

Only take this action when MS-DOS is not responding properly, or when the keyboard locks, preventing data from being entered.

HARD DRIVE (C:)

This drive is used to store your MS-DOS system files, application programs, data files, utilities, etc.

FLOPPY DRIVES (A: AND B:)

These drives are used to transfer new programs to your hard disk. They are also used to backup data files created on your hard disk.

If your computer has only one floppy drive, it is called A:

**Using the
Command
Prompt**

**Getting
Started**

Managing
Your
Directories

Managing
Your
Files

Managing
Your
Floppy Disks

Managing
Your
Hard Disk

CHANGE THE TIME

```
C> TIME
Current time is  9:16:08.11a
Enter new time: 16:30_
```

1 Type **TIME** and press
Enter. The time prompt
appears.

2 If the current time is
correct, press **Enter**.

3 If the time is incorrect,
type the new time
(example: **16:30**) and
press **Enter**.

*Note: You can type 4:30 p.m..
as either **16:30** or **4:30p** (with
no spaces between the 0 and
p). If you leave out the **p**,
MS-DOS assumes the time
is 4:30 a.m.*

VERIFY THE TIME

```
C>TIME
Current time is  9:16:08.11a
Enter new time:  16:30

C> TIME
Current time is  4:30:05.36p
Enter new time:

C>_
```

■ The command prompt
C> appears.

4 Type **TIME** and press
Enter. The new time
appears for your
verification.

5 To return to the
command prompt **C>**,
press **Enter**.

*Note: Most computers contain
a battery that keeps the
current date or time even
when the computer is off.*

*The Date and Time com-
mands are used to check or
change the date and time
currently set in the computer.*

CLEAR THE SCREEN

```
C>TIME
Current time is  9:16:08.11a
Enter new time:  16:30

C> TIME
Current time is  4:30:05.36p
Enter new time:

C> CLS_
```

1 Type **CLS** and press
Enter.

```
C> _
```

■ The screen is cleared.

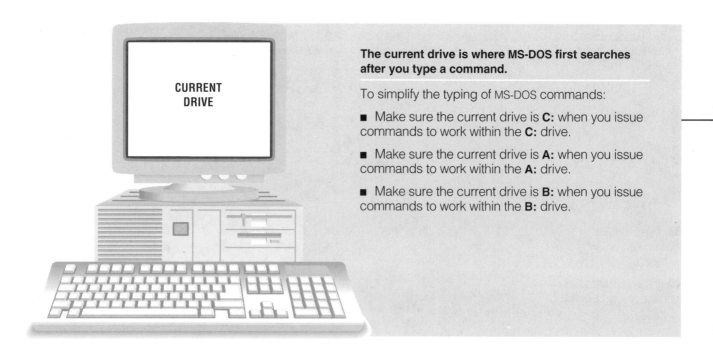

The current drive is where MS-DOS first searches after you type a command.

To simplify the typing of MS-DOS commands:

■ Make sure the current drive is **C:** when you issue commands to work within the **C:** drive.

■ Make sure the current drive is **A:** when you issue commands to work within the **A:** drive.

■ Make sure the current drive is **B:** when you issue commands to work within the **B:** drive.

SPECIFY A DIFFERENT DIRECTORY

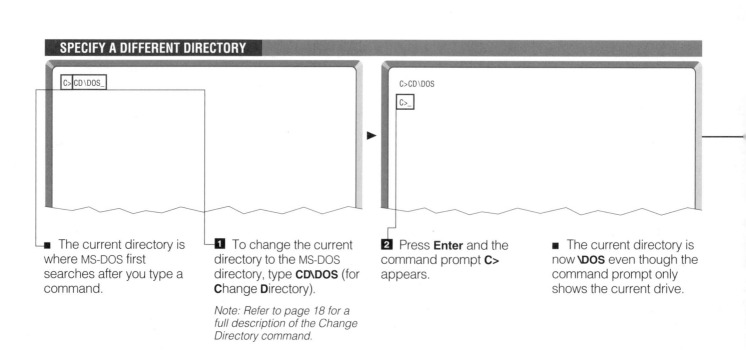

■ The current directory is where MS-DOS first searches after you type a command.

1 To change the current directory to the MS-DOS directory, type **CD\DOS** (for **C**hange **D**irectory).

Note: Refer to page 18 for a full description of the Change Directory command.

2 Press **Enter** and the command prompt **C>** appears.

■ The current directory is now **\DOS** even though the command prompt only shows the current drive.

Using this
Guide

Introduction
to MS-DOS 5.0

Change Date
or Time

Specify Drives
and Directories

Internal and External
Commands

Help

SPECIFY A DIFFERENT DRIVE

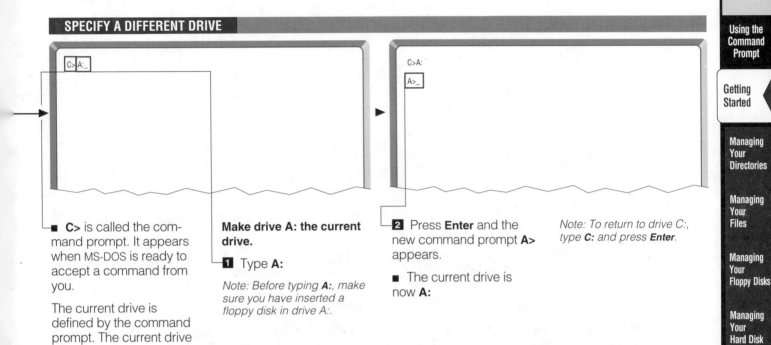

■ **C>** is called the command prompt. It appears when MS-DOS is ready to accept a command from you.

The current drive is defined by the command prompt. The current drive is **C:**

Make drive A: the current drive.

1 Type **A:**

*Note: Before typing **A:**, make sure you have inserted a floppy disk in drive A:.*

2 Press **Enter** and the new command prompt **A>** appears.

■ The current drive is now **A:**

*Note: To return to drive C:, type **C:** and press **Enter**.*

CHANGE THE SYSTEM PROMPT TO DISPLAY BOTH THE CURRENT DRIVE AND DIRECTORY

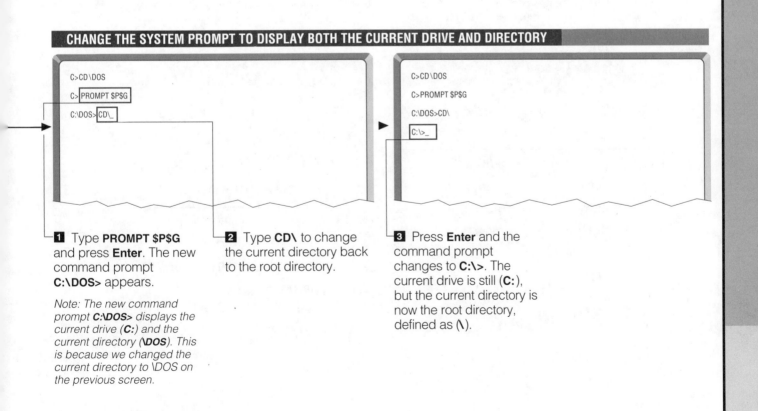

1 Type **PROMPT PG** and press **Enter**. The new command prompt **C:\DOS>** appears.

*Note: The new command prompt **C:\DOS>** displays the current drive (**C:**) and the current directory (**\DOS**). This is because we changed the current directory to \DOS on the previous screen.*

2 Type **CD** to change the current directory back to the root directory.

3 Press **Enter** and the command prompt changes to **C:\>**. The current drive is still (**C:**), but the current directory is now the root directory, defined as (****).

Using the Command Prompt

Getting Started

Managing Your Directories

Managing Your Files

Managing Your Floppy Disks

Managing Your Hard Disk

◀ 9

INTERNAL AND EXTERNAL COMMANDS

INTERNAL MS-DOS COMMANDS

EXTERNAL MS-DOS COMMANDS

Internal commands are part of an MS-DOS file called COMMAND.COM. This file (or program) is automatically loaded into your computer's internal or active memory when you start MS-DOS. Since all internal commands are resident in active memory, you can issue them from any drive or directory.

Note: Active memory is also called RAM (Random Access Memory). It is very fast, but volatile. When you turn off the computer, data stored in RAM is lost.

External commands are separate files (or programs) which reside on your hard drive or floppy disk. They are not kept in active or internal memory, thus the name external. To execute an external command, the computer must read the file (or program) from a directory or floppy disk. However, if the current drive and directory does not contain the MS-DOS file (or program), the computer will not find it.

To issue external commands from any drive or directory, a path command to the MS-DOS files (or programs) must be included. Refer to the next page for details.

Internal Commands	
CD	PROMPT
CLS	REN
COPY	RD
DATE	TIME
DELETE	TYPE
DIR	VER
MD	VOL
PATH	

External Commands	
BACKUP	RESTORE
CHKDSK	SORT
DISKCOPY	TREE
FORMAT	UNDELETE
MORE	XCOPY
PRINT	

**Using the
Command
Prompt**

**Getting
Started**

**Managing
Your
Directories**

**Managing
Your
Files**

**Managing
Your
Floppy Disks**

**Managing
Your
Hard Disk**

SPECIFY A SEARCH PATH

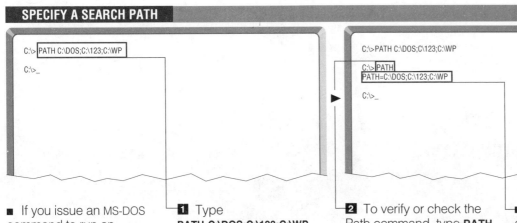

```
C:\> PATH C:\DOS;C:\123;C:\WP

C:\>_
```

```
C:\>PATH C:\DOS;C:\123;C:\WP

C:\> PATH
PATH=C:\DOS;C:\123;C:\WP

C:\>_
```

■ If you issue an MS-DOS command to run an application program (example: **Lotus 1-2-3**) or an external command (example: **FORMAT**), MS-DOS looks for the application program or external command in the current directory.

■ If the application program or external command is not in the current drive and directory, it will not start (or run).

■ The path command solves this problem by specifying a search path to allow MS-DOS to find an application program or external command that is not in the current drive and directory.

■ To make the Path command search more than one directory, you must specify several paths separated by semicolons (example: **PATH C:\DOS;C:\123**).

1 Type **PATH C:\DOS;C:\123;C:\WP** and press **Enter**.

■ You can now run external commands or applications such as Lotus 1-2-3 and WordPerfect from any drive or directory.

Note: To cancel the current path, type **PATH ;** *and press* **Enter**. *The path information is lost when the computer is turned off.*

2 To verify or check the Path command, type **PATH** and press **Enter**.

■ The current Path command is displayed.

Note: During the installation of MS-DOS 5.0 the path C:\DOS is automatically installed in your AUTOEXEC.BAT file.

The AUTOEXEC.BAT file allows you full control over the settings and tasks the computer executes each time it starts.

To add other paths to the AUTOEXEC.BAT file (example: C:\123 and C:\WP), refer to your Microsoft MS-DOS 5.0 User's Manual.

When you start your computer, MS-DOS searches the root directory of the default drive (usually A:). If the A: drive is open, MS-DOS proceeds to search the root directory of drive C:

DISPLAY THE MS-DOS VERSION NUMBER

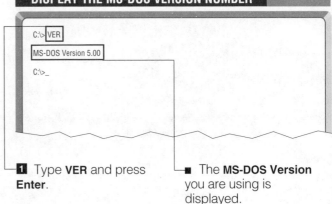

```
C:\> VER
MS-DOS Version 5.00

C:\>_
```

1 Type **VER** and press **Enter**.

■ The **MS-DOS Version** you are using is displayed.

HELP

1 To get Online Help on a specific MS-DOS command (example: **DIR**), type **DIR/?** or **HELP DIR**.

2 Press **Enter**.

`C:\> DIR/?`

MS-DOS COMMANDS DESCRIBED IN THIS GUIDE:

BACKUP	PRINT
CD	PROMPT
CHKDSK	RD
CLS	REN
COPY	RESTORE
DATE	SORT
DELETE	TIME
DIR	TREE
DISKCOPY	TYPE
FORMAT	UNDELETE
MD	VER
MORE	VOL
PATH	XCOPY

*Using this
Guide*

*Introduction
to MS-DOS 5.0*

*Change Date
or Time*

*Specify Drives
and Directories*

*Internal and External
Commands*

Help

**Using the
Command
Prompt**

**Getting
Started**

**Managing
Your
Directories**

**Managing
Your
Files**

**Managing
Your
Floppy Disks**

**Managing
Your
Hard Disk**

*Note: To display a listing
of all MS-DOS commands,
type **HELP** and press
Enter.*

*Each command includes a
short description of how it
works.*

*After **---More---** appears,
press any key to continue.*

```
Displays a list of files and subdirectories in a directory.

DIR [drive:][path][filename] [/P] [/W] [/A[[:]attributes]]
   [/O[[:]sortorder]] [/S] [/B] [/L]

   [drive:][path][filename]
               Specifies drive, directory, and/or files to list.
   /P          Pauses after each screenful of information.
   /W          Uses wide list format.
   /A          Displays files with specified attributes.
   attributes  D  Directories        R  Read-only files
               H  Hidden files       A  Files ready for archiving
               S  System files       -  Prefix meaning "not"
   /O          List by files in sorted order.
   sortorder   N  By name (alphabetic)   S  By size (smallest first)
               E  By extension (alphabetic) D  By date & time (earliest first)
               G  Group directories first   -  Prefix to reverse order
   /S          Displays files in specified directory and all subdirectories.
   /B          Uses bare format (no heading information or summary).
   /L          Uses lowercase.

Switches may be preset in the DIRCMD environment variable.  Override
preset switches by prefixing any switch with - (hypen)—for example, /-W.

C:\>PROMPT /?_
```

■ Help information is
displayed on **DIR**
(Directory).

3 To get information on
PROMPT, type **PROMPT/?**
and press **Enter**.

```
Changes the MS-DOS command prompt.

PROMPT [text]

   text       Specifies a new command prompt.

Prompt can be made up of normal characters and the following special codes:

   $Q    = (equal sign)
   $$    $ (dollar sign)
   $T    Current time
   $D    Current date
   $P    Current drive and path
   $V    MS-DOS version number
   $N    Current drive
   $G    > (greater-than sign)
   $L    < (less-than sign)
   $B    | (pipe)
   $H    Backspace (erases previous character)
   $E    Escape code (ASCII code 27)
   $_    Carriage return and linefeed

Type PROMPT without parameters to reset the prompt to the default setting.

C:\>_
```

■ Help is displayed on
PROMPT.

*Example: To change the
command prompt from **C>**
to **C:\>**, type **PROMPT PG**
and press **Enter**. The new
command prompt becomes
C:\>.*

FILES AND DIRECTORIES

In an efficient and productive office environment, people create, edit, review and organize paper documents (example: letters, worksheets, reports, etc.). These documents are stored in folders, which in turn are placed in cabinets. To retrieve a specific document, you must identify it (by name) and by location (cabinet and folder).

Computers work the same way. After creating a document, it must be named and saved. During the save process, you must tell MS-DOS the directory (folder) and drive (cabinet) the file is to reside in.

Note: A file is a document that has been saved.

MS-DOS lets you create a multilevel directory filing system to store and retrieve your files. The first level of this directory structure is called the root directory. From this directory other subdirectories can be created. A typical multilevel filing system is illustrated on the next page.

Note: The terms "directory" and "subdirectory" are used interchangeably. The "root directory" is the only "directory" that cannot be called a "subdirectory".

FILE SPECIFICATION

A file is specified by describing its drive, path and name (filename and extension).

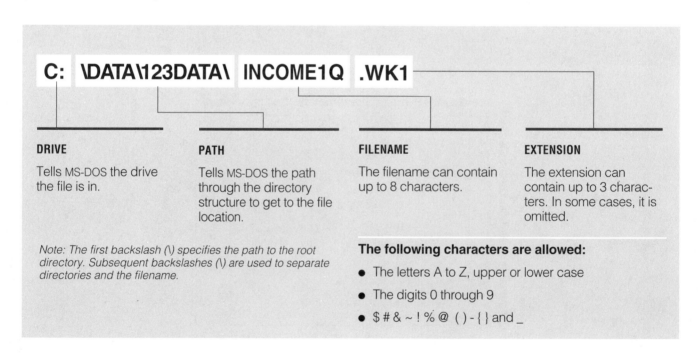

DRIVE

Tells MS-DOS the drive the file is in.

PATH

Tells MS-DOS the path through the directory structure to get to the file location.

Note: The first backslash (\) specifies the path to the root directory. Subsequent backslashes (\) are used to separate directories and the filename.

FILENAME

The filename can contain up to 8 characters.

EXTENSION

The extension can contain up to 3 characters. In some cases, it is omitted.

The following characters are allowed:

- The letters A to Z, upper or lower case
- The digits 0 through 9
- $ # & ~ ! % @ ( ) - { } and _

USING DIRECTORIES TO ORGANIZE YOUR FILES

Using the Command Prompt

Getting Started

Managing Your Directories

Managing Your Files

Managing Your Floppy Disks

Managing Your Hard Disk

Directories can contain files and/or paths to other directories (example: the root directory has paths to four subdirectories).

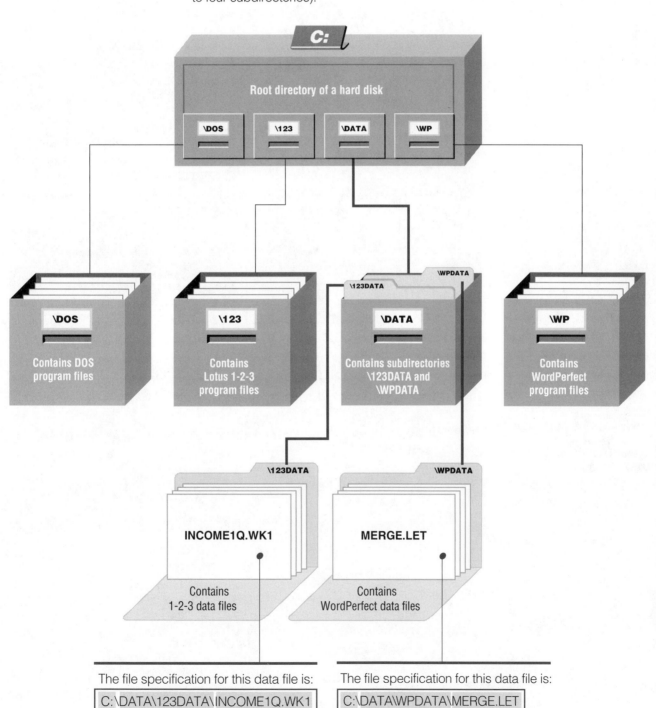

C:

Root directory of a hard disk

\DOS \123 \DATA \WP

\DOS
Contains DOS program files

\123
Contains Lotus 1-2-3 program files

\DATA
Contains subdirectories \123DATA and \WPDATA

\WP
Contains WordPerfect program files

\123DATA

\WPDATA

INCOME1Q.WK1
Contains 1-2-3 data files

MERGE.LET
Contains WordPerfect data files

The file specification for this data file is:

C:\DATA\123DATA\INCOME1Q.WK1

The file specification for this data file is:

C:\DATA\WPDATA\MERGE.LET

MAKE DIRECTORY

DIRECTORY ORGANIZATION

This chart illustrates how a company might organize their application programs and data files on a hard disk.

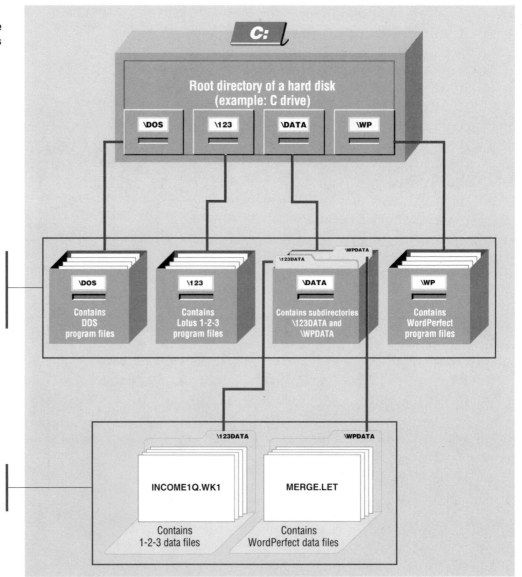

Subdirectories for MS-DOS, Data and Program files (example: Lotus 1-2-3 and WordPerfect 5.1) are created one level below the root directory.

Subdirectories for **123DATA** and **WPDATA** files are created one level below the **\DATA** directory.

In this directory organization, each program has its own directory. In addition, each program's data files has its own separate directory.

The separation of program files (example: **Lotus 1-2-3**) and their respective data files (example: **INCOME1Q.WK1**) improves your efficiency and productivity when working with large quantities of different kinds of information.

MAKE DIRECTORY

The Make Directory command (typed as MD) allows you to create a multilevel directory filing system.

The screen flow to the right describes how to create the **DATA** directory structure illustrated on the opposite page.

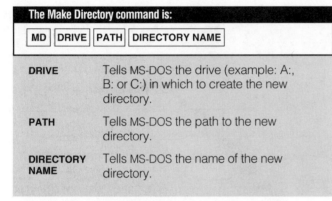

The Make Directory command is:			
MD	DRIVE	PATH	DIRECTORY NAME

DRIVE — Tells MS-DOS the drive (example: A:, B: or C:) in which to create the new directory.

PATH — Tells MS-DOS the path to the new directory.

DIRECTORY NAME — Tells MS-DOS the name of the new directory.

Note: If you omit the drive and path, new subdirectories are created in the current drive and within the current directory.

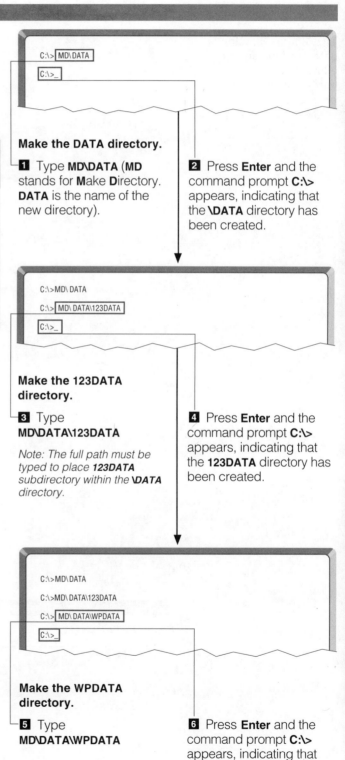

Make the DATA directory.

1 Type **MD\DATA** (MD stands for **M**ake **D**irectory. **DATA** is the name of the new directory).

2 Press **Enter** and the command prompt **C:\>** appears, indicating that the **\DATA** directory has been created.

Make the 123DATA directory.

3 Type **MD\DATA\123DATA**

*Note: The full path must be typed to place **123DATA** subdirectory within the **\DATA** directory.*

4 Press **Enter** and the command prompt **C:\>** appears, indicating that the **123DATA** directory has been created.

Make the WPDATA directory.

5 Type **MD\DATA\WPDATA**

6 Press **Enter** and the command prompt **C:\>** appears, indicating that the **WPDATA** directory has been created.

CHANGE DIRECTORY

The Change Directory command (typed as CD) allows you to change the current directory to any other directory.

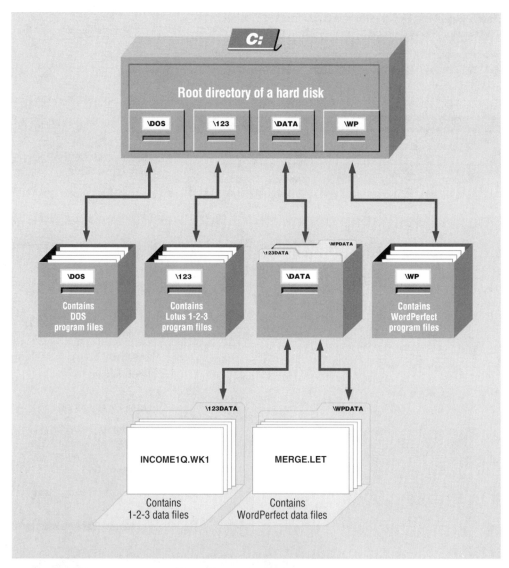

The Change Directory command is:		
CD	PATH	
PATH		Tells MS-DOS the path to the directory containing the file you want to view or run.

Using the
Command
Prompt

Getting
Started

Managing
Your
Directories

Managing
Your
Files

Managing
Your
Floppy Disks

Managing
Your
Hard Disk

CHANGE THE CURRENT DIRECTORY FROM C:\ TO C:\DATA\123DATA

C:\> CD\DATA\123DATA

C:\DATA\123DATA> DIR_

C:\>CD\DATA\123DATA

C:\DATA\123DATA>DIR

Volume in drive C is HARDDRIVE
Volume Serial Number is 1679-791B
Directory of C:\DATA\123DATA

```
.              <DIR>        07-01-91   10:04a
..             <DIR>        07-01-91   10:03a
INCOME1Q  WK1       5       07-15-91   1:31p
INCOME2Q  WK1       6       07-20-91   9:42a
JIM       WK1       1       08-02-91   3:47p
      5 file(s)               12 bytes
                         18821040 bytes free
```

1 Type **CD\DATA\123DATA** and press **Enter**.

■ The command prompt **C:\DATA\123DATA>** appears displaying the new current directory.

2 Type **DIR** and press **Enter** to display the current directory.

■ This line represents the current directory (example: **\DATA\123DATA**) and the date and time it was created.

■ This line represents the parent of the current directory (example: **\DATA**) and the date and time it was created.

Note: To create practice files, refer to page 21.

MOVE UP ONE DIRECTORY LEVEL (SHORTCUT)

C:\DATA\123DATA> CD ..

C:\DATA\123DATA>CD ..

C:\DATA>_

1 To move up one directory level from any directory, type **CD ..** and press **Enter**.

■ In this example we changed from directory **\DATA\123DATA** to directory **\DATA**.

Note: This is a fast method of moving up the directory structure one level at a time.

MOVE DOWN ONE DIRECTORY LEVEL (SHORTCUT)

C:\DATA> CD WPDATA_

C:\DATA>CD WPDATA

C:\DATA\WPDATA>_

1 To move down one directory level from any directory, type **CD <directory name>** (example: **CD WPDATA**), and press **Enter**.

■ In this example we changed from directory **\DATA** to directory **\DATA\WPDATA**.

Note: This is a fast method of moving down the directory structure one level at a time.

*Note: To change from any directory to the root directory, type **CD** and press **Enter**.*

REMOVE DIRECTORY

REMOVE DIRECTORY

The Remove Directory command (typed as RD) allows you to remove a directory from your multilevel filing structure.

Directories can only be removed starting from the bottom of the directory structure.

This is because a directory can only be removed when it does not contain files or other subdirectories.

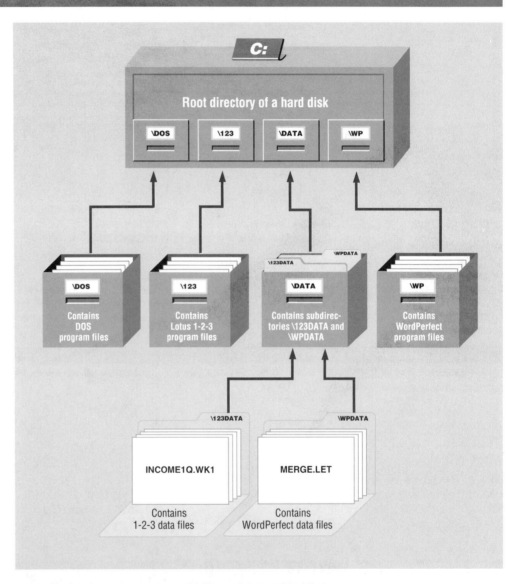

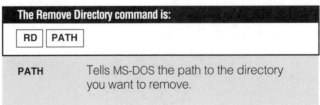

The Remove Directory command is:

RD	PATH

PATH   Tells MS-DOS the path to the directory you want to remove.

REMOVE A DIRECTORY

Using the Command Prompt

Getting Started

Managing Your Directories

Managing Your Files

Managing Your Floppy Disks

Managing Your Hard Disk

WHEN THE DIRECTORY DOES NOT CONTAIN FILES OR SUBDIRECTORIES

```
C:\>RD\DATA\123DATA
C:\>_
```

■ To change from any directory to the root directory type **CD** and press **Enter**.

1 To remove a directory (example: **123DATA** directory), type **RD\DATA\123DATA** and press **Enter**.

■ The command prompt **C:\>** appears indicating that the directory has been removed.

PRACTICE FILES

Normally, files are created using application software (such as word processing, spreadsheet, graphic packages, etc). The method below should only be used to create practice files.

You can create practice files for this and subsequent pages using the COPY FROM THE KEYBOARD feature described on page 35.

> **Example: Create a file named INCOME1Q.WK1 and save it to the \DATA\123DATA directory.**
>
> **1** To change the current directory to \DATA\123DATA, type **CD\DATA\123DATA** and press **Enter**.
>
> **2** Type **COPY CON INCOME1Q.WK1** and press **Enter**.
>
> **3** Type any character (example: A to Z). If you want the file to contain 2 bytes, type the character twice.
>
> **4** Press **F6** or **Ctrl-Z** (hold down **Ctrl** while you press **Z**). Press **Enter** and the file is copied to the \DATA\123DATA directory and named INCOME1Q.WK1.

WHEN THE DIRECTORY CONTAINS FILES OR SUBDIRECTORIES

```
C:\>RD\ DATA\123DATA
Invalid path, not directory,
or directory not empty
C:\>DIR \DATA\123DATA_
```

1 To remove the **123DATA** directory, type **RD\DATA\123DATA** and press **Enter**.

■ A message appears indicating that either files or directories exist within the **123DATA** directory.

2 Type **DIR \DATA\123DATA** and press **Enter**.

Note: Refer to page 24 for a full description of the Directory command.

```
C:\>RD\ DATA\123DATA
Invalid path, not directory,
or directory not empty

C:\>DIR\DATA\123DATA

Volume in drive C is HARDDRIVE
Volume Serial Number is 1679-791B
Directory of C:\DATA\123DATA

.               <DIR>        07-01-91  10:04a
..              <DIR>        07-01-91  10:03a
INCOME1Q  WK1         5      07-15-91   1:31p
INCOME2Q  WK1         6      07-20-91   9:42a
JIM       WK1         1      08-02-91   3:47p
        5 file(s)               12 bytes
                        18821040 bytes free

C:\>DEL \DATA\123DATA\*.*
All files in directory will be deleted!
Are you sure (Y/N)? Y_
```

3 To delete all files in the directory, type **DEL \DATA\123DATA*.*** and press **Enter**.

Note: Refer to page 38 for a full description of the Delete command.

4 Type **Y** and press **Enter** to delete the data files.

5 Repeat from Step **1** above to remove the empty directory.

TREE

The Tree command displays directories and subdirectories in a visually structured format.

Since Tree is an external command, the Path command should include C:\DOS. During the installation of MS-DOS 5.0, the Path command C:\DOS is automatically installed in your AUTOEXEC.BAT file.

Note: If for some reason the Path command C:\DOS is not installed in your AUTOEXEC.BAT file, the current drive and directory must be changed to C:\DOS before issuing this command (refer to page 8).

The Tree command is:

TREE	DRIVE	PATH	/F

DRIVE	Tells MS-DOS the drive (example: A:, B: or C:) of the directory structure to be displayed.
PATH	Tells MS-DOS where to begin displaying the directory structure.
/F	Tells MS-DOS to show all files in the displayed directories.

All examples in this guide are based on the directory structure illustrated below:

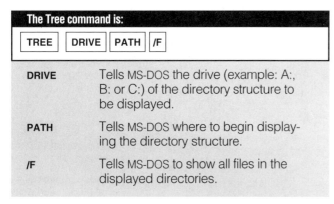

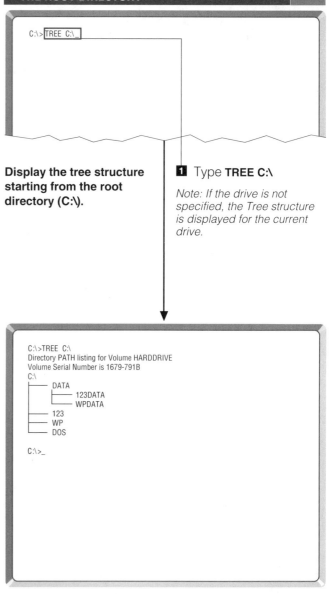

Display the tree structure starting from the root directory (C:\).

1 Type **TREE C:**

Note: If the drive is not specified, the Tree structure is displayed for the current drive.

2 Press **Enter** and the directory tree structure, starting from the root directory (**C:**), is displayed.

DISPLAY A TREE STRUCTURE STARTING FROM A SUBDIRECTORY AND INCLUDE ALL FILES

C:\> `TREE C:\DATA/F¦MORE_`

Display the tree structure starting from C:\DATA.

1 Type

TREE C:\DATA/F¦MORE

Note: Only add the **¦MORE** *command if you expect the display to exceed one screen. Hold down* **Shift** *while you press* **Backslash (\)** *to add* **¦** *to the command. Do* **not** *press the semi-colon key.*

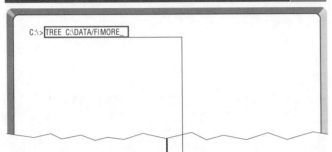

```
Directory PATH listing for Volume HARDDRIVE
Volume Serial Number is 1679-791B
C:\DATA
├──── 123DATA
│         INCOME1Q.WK1
│         INCOME2Q.WK1
│         INCOME3Q.WK1
│         INCOME4Q.WK1
│         JIM.WK1
│         PLAN1.WK1
│         PLAN2.WK1
│         PLAN3.WK1
│         PROJECT1.WK1
│         PROJECT2.WK1
│         PROJECT3.WK1
├──── WPDATA
          1QPROFIT.MEM
          2QPROFIT.MEM
          3QPROFIT.MEM
          DO_MON.LET
          DO_TUES.LET
          MERGE.LET
          NOTE1Q.TXT
– – More – –
```

2 Press **Enter** and the tree structure, including all directories and files starting from the **\DATA** directory, appear on the screen.

3 Press any key to display the next screen. Continue until all files and directories are displayed.

PRINT A TREE STRUCTURE STARTING FROM A SUBDIRECTORY AND INCLUDE ALL FILES

C:\> `TREE C:\DATA/F>PRN_`

Print the tree structure starting from C:\DATA.

1 Type

TREE C:\DATA/F>PRN and press **Enter**.

Note: **>PRN** *directs the output to your printer instead of the screen.*

```
Directory PATH listing for Volume HARDDRIVE
Volume Serial Number is 1679-791B
C:\DATA
├──── 123DATA
│         INCOME1Q.WK1
│         INCOME2Q.WK1
│         INCOME3Q.WK1
│         INCOME4Q.WK1
│         JIM.WK1
│         PLAN1.WK1
│         PLAN2.WK1
│         PLAN3.WK1
│         PROJECT1.WK1
│         PROJECT2.WK1
│         PROJECT3.WK1
├──── WPDATA
          1QPROFIT.MEM
          2QPROFIT.MEM
          3QPROFIT.MEM
          DO_MON.LET
          DO_TUE.LET
          MERGE.LET
          NOTE1Q.TXT
          NOTE2Q.TXT
          TEST.LET
          TRAINING.LET
```

Note: Refer to the printer manual to determine if your printer supports the extended character set. If it does not, type **/A** *after the Tree command (example:* **TREE C:\DATA/F/A>PRN**). *This adds vertical bars, hyphens, etc. to help draw the tree structure.*

Using the Command Prompt

Getting Started

Managing Your Directories ◀

Managing Your Files

Managing Your Floppy Disks

Managing Your Hard Disk

DIRECTORY

The Directory command (typed as DIR) lists all files in a directory, including information about their size and when they were created or last modified.

You can ask for a listing of all files in a directory, for some of them, or for a single file.

The Directory command is:			
DIR	DRIVE	PATH	FILENAME AND EXTENSION

DRIVE	Tells MS-DOS the drive (example: A:, B: or C:) containing the directory to be displayed.
PATH	Tells MS-DOS the path to the directory containing the files to be displayed.
FILENAME AND EXTENSION	Tells MS-DOS the filenames and extensions to be displayed.

Note: When the drive and path are not specified, MS-DOS displays the directory in the current drive and directory.

When a filename and extension are not specified, MS-DOS displays all the files in the directory.

LIST ALL FILES IN A DIRECTORY

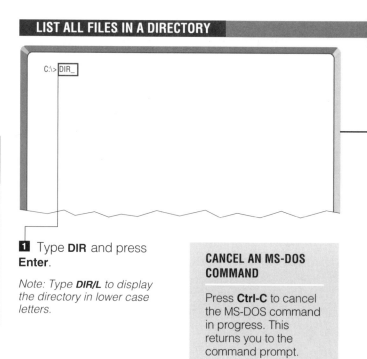

1 Type **DIR** and press **Enter**.

*Note: Type **DIR/L** to display the directory in lower case letters.*

CANCEL AN MS-DOS COMMAND

Press **Ctrl-C** to cancel the MS-DOS command in progress. This returns you to the command prompt.

LIST ONE FILE IN A DIRECTORY

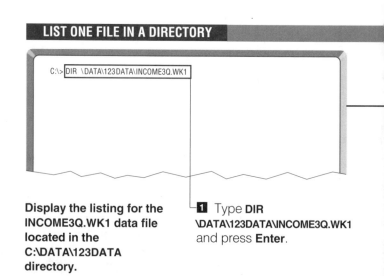

Display the listing for the INCOME3Q.WK1 data file located in the C:\DATA\123DATA directory.

1 Type **DIR \DATA\123DATA\INCOME3Q.WK1** and press **Enter**.

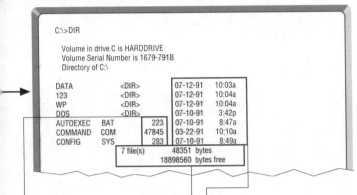

```
C:\>DIR

    Volume in drive C is HARDDRIVE
    Volume Serial Number is 1679-791B
    Directory of C:\

DATA          <DIR>          07-12-91    10:03a
123           <DIR>          07-12-91    10:04a
WP            <DIR>          07-12-91    10:04a
DOS           <DIR>          07-10-91     3:42p
AUTOEXEC  BAT      223       07-10-91     8:47a
COMMAND   COM    47845       03-22-91    10:10a
CONFIG    SYS      283       07-10-91     8:49a
        7 file(s)          48351  bytes
                        18898560  bytes free
```

■ A listing of all files in the root directory is displayed.

■ This column lists the amount of space each file contains in bytes. A byte is one character.

■ The date and time files were created or last modified.

■ The total number of files in the directory and the amount of space still available on the disk are listed.

MS-DOS EDITING KEYS

Tab	The cursor moves to the next tab stop.
Backspace	Moves the cursor back one tab stop or deletes a single character to the left of the cursor.
Esc	The current line is cancelled.

The computer remembers the last MS-DOS command typed. The command can then be recalled or modified using the F1, F2, or F3 editing keys.

F1	Displays one character at a time from the last line you entered.
F2	Displays the last line entered up to, but not including, a specified character (example: if the last line entered was **DIR AUTOEXEC.BAT** and you pressed **F2**, and then **E**, the screen would display **DIR AUTO**).
F3	Displays the last line entered, or what remains, if it has been partially edited.

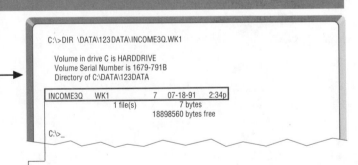

```
C:\>DIR \DATA\123DATA\INCOME3Q.WK1

    Volume in drive C is HARDDRIVE
    Volume Serial Number is 1679-791B
    Directory of C:\DATA\123DATA

INCOME3Q   WK1           7    07-18-91    2:34p
        1 file(s)            7 bytes
                      18898560 bytes free

C:\>_
```

■ MS-DOS displays the **INCOME3Q.WK1** data file listing.

Note: To create practice files, refer to page 21.

Note: One kilobyte of data contains 1,024 bytes, and one megabyte represents 1,048,576 bytes. A typical page of double spaced text contains approximately 1,500 bytes (characters of data).

Using the Command Prompt

Getting Started

Managing Your Directories

Managing Your Files

Managing Your Floppy Disks

Managing Your Hard Disk

DIRECTORY

PAGE DISPLAY /P

When a directory contains more than one screen of files, the Directory command automatically scrolls to the end of the directory listing.

To view all the files in the directory one screen at a time, the /P (for Page display) parameter is used.

TO DISPLAY DIRECTORIES ONLY	TO DISPLAY FILES ONLY
Type **DIR/AD**.	Type **DIR/A-D**.

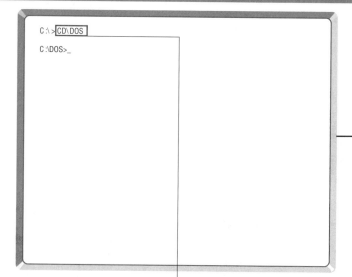

Display a directory (example: the **\DOS** directory) one screen at a time.

1 Type **CD\DOS** and press **Enter** to change the current directory to the **\DOS** directory.

WIDE DISPLAY /W

To view a directory containing a large number of files across the screen instead of down, the /W (for Wide display) parameter is used.

*Note: The /P and /W options can be used together by typing **DIR/P/W** or **DIR/W/P**.*

*To display only files in the wide display mode, type **DIR/W/A-D**.*

Display a directory (example: the **\DOS** directory) in the wide display mode.

1 Type **DIR/W** and press **Enter**.

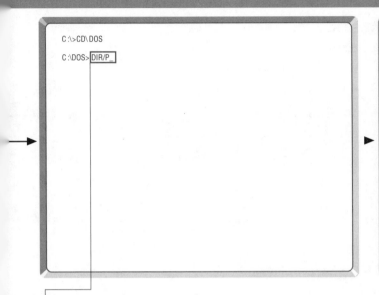

2 Type **DIR/P** and press **Enter**.

■ MS-DOS displays the first screen of files.

3 Press any key to view the second screen of files. Continue until all files have been displayed.

*Note: To print the directory, type **DIR>PRN** and press **Enter**.*

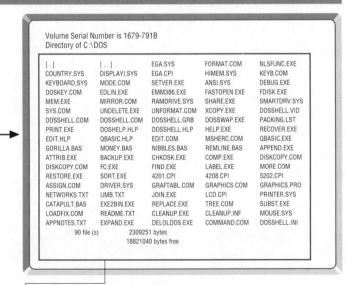

■ MS-DOS displays the directory in wide display format.

Note: To pack more information into the display, the file size and creation date are omitted.

OTHER WAYS TO HALT THE DISPLAY FROM SCROLLING

CTRL-S

Press **Ctrl-S** to temporarily freeze the screen display. Press any key to continue. You can repeat this process until you reach the end of the screen display.

PAUSE

Press **Pause** to temporarily freeze the screen display. Press any key to continue. You can repeat this process until you reach the end of the screen display.

Using the Command Prompt

Getting Started

Managing Your Directories

Managing Your Files

Managing Your Floppy Disks

Managing Your Hard Disk

◀ 27

DIRECTORY

USING THE ? WILDCARD

When you use a ? (question mark) in a filename or extension within an MS-DOS command, the ? is interpreted to mean any character in that position.

This is useful for finding files with similar names.

Note: To create practice files refer to page 21. Make sure you save your files to A:\ (the root directory of the floppy disk in drive A:) for the example on these two pages.

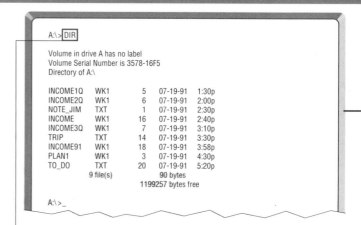

```
A:\>DIR

Volume in drive A has no label
Volume Serial Number is 3578-16F5
Directory of A:\

INCOME1Q    WK1      5    07-19-91    1:30p
INCOME2Q    WK1      6    07-19-91    2:00p
NOTE_JIM    TXT      1    07-19-91    2:30p
INCOME      WK1     16    07-19-91    2:40p
INCOME3Q    WK1      7    07-19-91    3:10p
TRIP        TXT     14    07-19-91    3:30p
INCOME91    WK1     18    07-19-91    3:58p
PLAN1       WK1      3    07-19-91    4:30p
TO_DO       TXT     20    07-19-91    5:20p
         9 file(s)           90 bytes
                      1199257 bytes free

A:\>_
```

1 Type **DIR** and press **Enter** to display all the files in floppy disk A:

*Note: Type **A:** and press **Enter** to change the current drive from **C:** to **A:**

USING THE * WILDCARD

When you use an * (asterisk) in a filename or extension within an MS-DOS command, the * is interpreted to mean any number of characters, from one character up to an entire filename or extension.

This is useful for finding files containing groups of characters (example: INCOME, NOTE, TRIP, WK1 etc.).

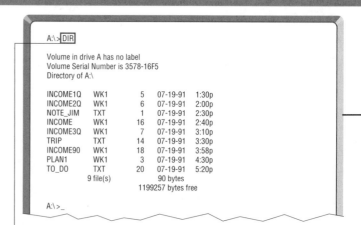

```
A:\>DIR

Volume in drive A has no label
Volume Serial Number is 3578-16F5
Directory of A:\

INCOME1Q    WK1      5    07-19-91    1:30p
INCOME2Q    WK1      6    07-19-91    2:00p
NOTE_JIM    TXT      1    07-19-91    2:30p
INCOME      WK1     16    07-19-91    2:40p
INCOME3Q    WK1      7    07-19-91    3:10p
TRIP        TXT     14    07-19-91    3:30p
INCOME90    WK1     18    07-19-91    3:58p
PLAN1       WK1      3    07-19-91    4:30p
TO_DO       TXT     20    07-19-91    5:20p
         9 file(s)           90 bytes
                      1199257 bytes free

A:\>_
```

1 Type **DIR** and press **Enter** to display all the files in floppy disk A:

*Note: Typing **DIR** is equivalent to typing **DIR** *.**

Using the Command Prompt

Getting Started

Managing Your Directories

Managing Your Files ◀

Managing Your Floppy Disks

Managing Your Hard Disk

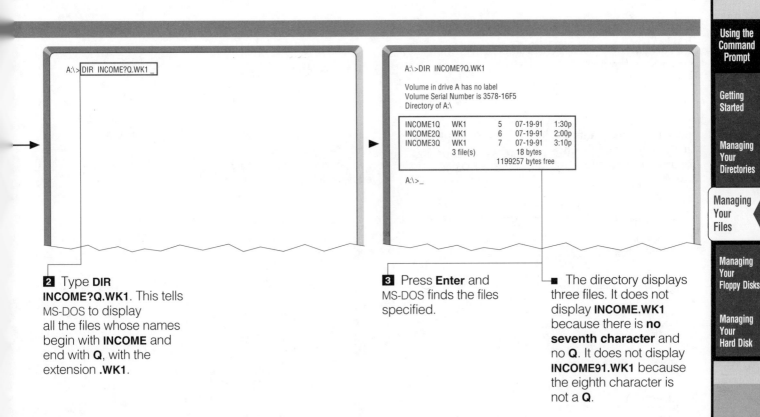

2 Type **DIR INCOME?Q.WK1**. This tells MS-DOS to display all the files whose names begin with **INCOME** and end with **Q**, with the extension **.WK1**.

3 Press **Enter** and MS-DOS finds the files specified.

■ The directory displays three files. It does not display **INCOME.WK1** because there is **no seventh character** and no **Q**. It does not display **INCOME91.WK1** because the eighth character is not a **Q**.

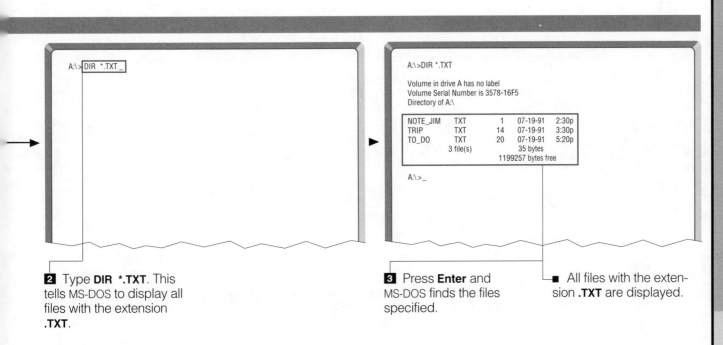

2 Type **DIR *.TXT**. This tells MS-DOS to display all files with the extension **.TXT**.

3 Press **Enter** and MS-DOS finds the files specified.

■ All files with the extension **.TXT** are displayed.

SORT
FILES

SORT A DIRECTORY BY NAME

C:\DOS> DIR/ON¦MORE_

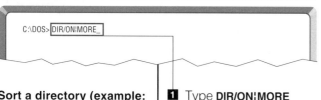

Sort a directory (example: \DOS) by name in ascending order (1 to 9 and A to Z).

1 Type **DIR/ON¦MORE**

Note: Type ***CD\DOS*** *and press* ***Enter*** *to change the current directory to* ***\DOS***.

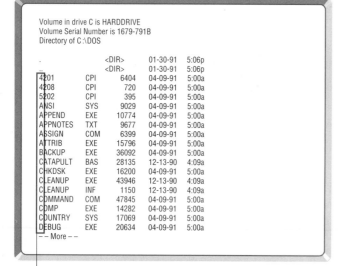

```
Volume in drive C is HARDDRIVE
Volume Serial Number is 1679-791B
Directory of C:\DOS

.               <DIR>      01-30-91    5:06p
..              <DIR>      01-30-91    5:06p
4201    CPI      6404      04-09-91    5:00a
4208    CPI       720      04-09-91    5:00a
5202    CPI       395      04-09-91    5:00a
ANSI    SYS      9029      04-09-91    5:00a
APPEND  EXE     10774      04-09-91    5:00a
APPNOTES TXT     9677      04-09-91    5:00a
ASSIGN  COM      6399      04-09-91    5:00a
ATTRIB  EXE     15796      04-09-91    5:00a
BACKUP  EXE     36092      04-09-91    5:00a
CATAPULT BAS    28135      12-13-90    4:09a
CHKDSK  EXE     16200      04-09-91    5:00a
CLEANUP EXE     43946      12-13-90    4:09a
CLEANUP INF      1150      12-13-90    4:09a
COMMAND COM     47845      04-09-91    5:00a
COMP    EXE     14282      04-09-91    5:00a
COUNTRY SYS     17069      04-09-91    5:00a
DEBUG   EXE     20634      04-09-91    5:00a
-- More --
```

2 Press **Enter** to display the files sorted by filename.

Note: Adding **¦MORE** *to the Directory command displays one screen of files at a time.*

3 Press any key to display more files.

SORT A DIRECTORY BY EXTENSION

C:\DOS> DIR/OE¦MORE_

Sort a directory (example: \DOS) by extension in ascending order (1 to 9 and A to Z).

1 Type **DIR/OE¦MORE**

```
Volume in drive C is HARDDRIVE
Volume Serial Number is 1679-791B
Directory of C:\DOS

.                <DIR>     01-30-91    5:06p
..               <DIR>     01-30-91    5:06p
GORILLA   BAS   29434      04-09-91    5:00a
MONEY     BAS   46225      04-09-91    5:00a
NIBBLES   BAS   24103      04-09-91    5:00a
REMLINE   BAS   12314      04-09-91    5:00a
CATAPULT  BAS   28135      04-09-91    5:00a
FORMAT    COM   32945      04-09-91    5:00a
KEYB      COM   14986      04-09-91    5:00a
MODE      COM   23537      04-09-91    5:00a
DOSKEY    COM    5883      04-09-91    5:00a
MIRROR    COM   18169      04-09-91    5:00a
SYS       COM   13440      04-09-91    5:00a
UNFORMAT  COM   18576      04-09-91    5:00a
DOSSHELL  COM    4623      04-09-91    5:00a
EDIT      COM     413      04-09-91    5:00a
MSHERC    COM    6934      04-09-91    5:00a
DISKCOMP  COM   10652      04-09-91    5:00a
DISCOPY   COM   11793      04-09-91    5:00a
-- More --
```

2 Press **Enter** to display the files sorted by extension.

3 Press any key to display more files.

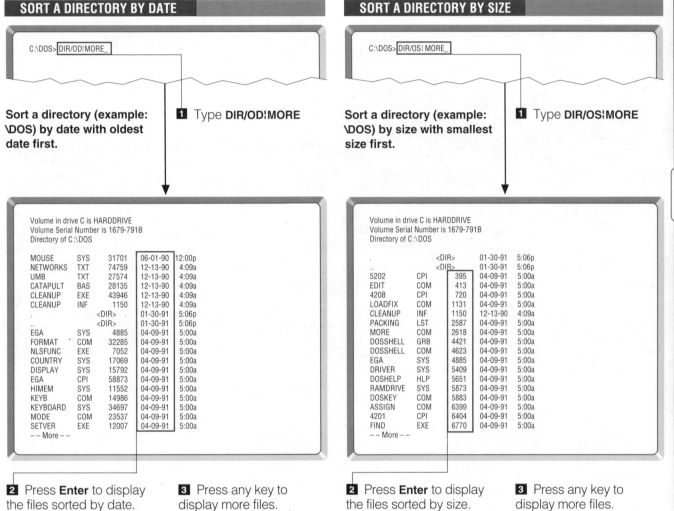

SORT A DIRECTORY BY DATE

C:\DOS> `DIR/OD¦MORE_`

Sort a directory (example: \DOS) by date with oldest date first.

1 Type **DIR/OD¦MORE**

```
Volume in drive C is HARDDRIVE
Volume Serial Number is 1679-791B
Directory of C:\DOS

MOUSE     SYS   31701   06-01-90   12:00p
NETWORKS  TXT   74759   12-13-90   4:09a
UMB       TXT   27574   12-13-90   4:09a
CATAPULT  BAS   28135   12-13-90   4:09a
CLEANUP   EXE   43946   12-13-90   4:09a
CLEANUP   INF    1150   12-13-90   4:09a
.              <DIR>    01-30-91   5:06p
..             <DIR>    01-30-91   5:06p
EGA       SYS    4885   04-09-91   5:00a
FORMAT    COM   32285   04-09-91   5:00a
NLSFUNC   EXE    7052   04-09-91   5:00a
COUNTRY   SYS   17069   04-09-91   5:00a
DISPLAY   SYS   15792   04-09-91   5:00a
EGA       CPI   58873   04-09-91   5:00a
HIMEM     SYS   11552   04-09-91   5:00a
KEYB      COM   14986   04-09-91   5:00a
KEYBOARD  SYS   34697   04-09-91   5:00a
MODE      COM   23537   04-09-91   5:00a
SETVER    EXE   12007   04-09-91   5:00a
– – More – –
```

2 Press **Enter** to display the files sorted by date.

3 Press any key to display more files.

SORT A DIRECTORY BY SIZE

C:\DOS> `DIR/OS¦MORE_`

Sort a directory (example: \DOS) by size with smallest size first.

1 Type **DIR/OS¦MORE**

```
Volume in drive C is HARDDRIVE
Volume Serial Number is 1679-791B
Directory of C:\DOS

.              <DIR>    01-30-91   5:06p
..             <DIR>    01-30-91   5:06p
5202      CPI     395   04-09-91   5:00a
EDIT      COM     413   04-09-91   5:00a
4208      CPI     720   04-09-91   5:00a
LOADFIX   COM    1131   04-09-91   5:00a
CLEANUP   INF    1150   12-13-90   4:09a
PACKING   LST    2587   04-09-91   5:00a
MORE      COM    2618   04-09-91   5:00a
DOSSHELL  GRB    4421   04-09-91   5:00a
DOSSHELL  COM    4623   04-09-91   5:00a
EGA       SYS    4885   04-09-91   5:00a
DRIVER    SYS    5409   04-09-91   5:00a
DOSHELP   HLP    5651   04-09-91   5:00a
RAMDRIVE  SYS    5873   04-09-91   5:00a
DOSKEY    COM    5883   04-09-91   5:00a
ASSIGN    COM    6399   04-09-91   5:00a
4201      CPI    6404   04-09-91   5:00a
FIND      EXE    6770   04-09-91   5:00a
– – More – –
```

2 Press **Enter** to display the files sorted by size.

3 Press any key to display more files.

SORT IN REVERSE ORDER AND PAUSE EVERY SCREEN

SORT BY	TYPE
Name	DIR/O-N¦MORE
Extension	DIR/O-E¦MORE
Date	DIR/O-D¦MORE
Size	DIR/O-S¦MORE

SORT AND SEND DIRECTLY TO THE PRINTER

SORT BY	TYPE
Name	DIR/ON >PRN
Extension	DIR/OE >PRN
Date	DIR/OD >PRN
Size	DIR/OS >PRN

Using the Command Prompt

Getting Started

Managing Your Directories

Managing Your Files

Managing Your Floppy Disks

Managing Your Hard Disk

◀ 31

COPY FILES

The Copy command lets you make duplicates of your files and save them to a different drive/directory or to the same drive/directory.

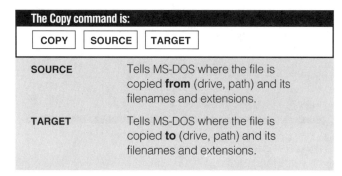

The Copy command is:
COPY   SOURCE   TARGET

SOURCE	Tells MS-DOS where the file is copied **from** (drive, path) and its filenames and extensions.
TARGET	Tells MS-DOS where the file is copied **to** (drive, path) and its filenames and extensions.

Note: Always change the current drive and directory to where the source file is located.

If the drive is not included in the source or target, copying takes place in the current drive.

If the path is not included in the source or target, copying takes place in the current directory.

If filenames and extensions are not included in the target, the filenames and extensions from the source are copied to the target.

from drive C: to drive A: using the same name

Suppose you have a file named **JIM.WK1** in the **C:\DATA\123DATA** directory and want to copy it to the root directory of the floppy disk in drive A:

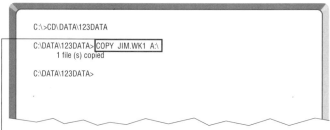

```
C:\>CD\DATA\123DATA

C:\DATA\123DATA> COPY  JIM.WK1  A:\
        1 file (s) copied

C:\DATA\123DATA>
```

1 Change the current directory to where the source file is located (example: type **CD\DATA\123DATA** and press **Enter**).

2 To copy **JIM.WK1** to the root directory of the floppy disk in drive A:, type:

COPY | JIM.WK1 | A:\
       Source   Target

and press **Enter**.

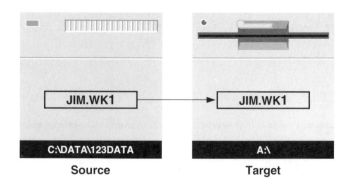

JIM.WK1 → JIM.WK1
C:\DATA\123DATA — A:\
Source — Target

This command copies JIM.WK1 **from** C:\DATA\123DATA (the source), **to** JIM.WK1 in the root directory of the floppy disk in drive A: (the target).

Using the Command Prompt

Getting Started

Managing Your Directories

Managing Your Files

Managing Your Floppy Disks

Managing Your Hard Disk

from drive C: to drive A: using a different name

Suppose you have a file named JIM.WK1 in the C:\DATA\123DATA directory and you want to copy it to the root directory of the floppy disk in drive A: and name it NOTE1.WK1.

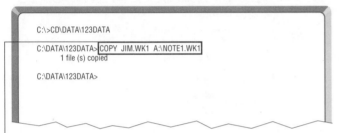

```
C:\>CD\DATA\123DATA

C:\DATA\123DATA> COPY JIM.WK1 A:\NOTE1.WK1
          1 file (s) copied

C:\DATA\123DATA>
```

1 Change the current directory to where the source file is located (example: type **CD\DATA\123DATA** and press **Enter**).

2 To copy **JIM.WK1** to the root directory of the floppy disk in drive A:, with a new filename, type:

COPY JIM.WK1 A:\NOTE1.WK1
     Source   Target

and press **Enter**.

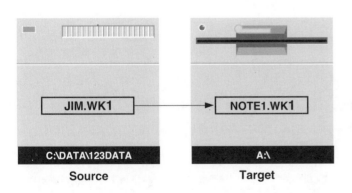

JIM.WK1 → NOTE1.WK1

C:\DATA\123DATA — **Source**   A:\ — **Target**

This command copies JIM.WK1 **from** C:\DATA\123DATA (the source), **to** NOTE1.WK1 in the root directory of the floppy disk in drive A: (the target).

from drive A: to drive C: using the * wildcard

Suppose you want to copy several worksheets (example: INCOME1Q.WK1, INCOME2Q.WK1 and INCOME3Q.WK1) from the root directory of the floppy disk in drive A: to the C:\DATA\123DATA directory.

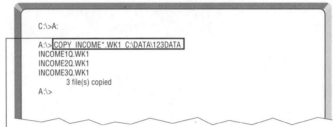

```
C:\>A:

A:\> COPY INCOME*.WK1 C:\DATA\123DATA
INCOME1Q.WK1
INCOME2Q.WK1
INCOME3Q.WK1
          3 file(s) copied
A:\>
```

1 Type **A:** and press **Enter** to change the current drive to A:

2 To copy the **INCOME worksheets** to C:\DATA\123DATA, type:

COPY INCOME*.WK1 C:\DATA\123DATA
     Source   Target

and press **Enter**.

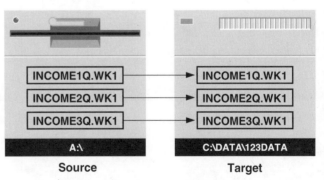

INCOME1Q.WK1 → INCOME1Q.WK1
INCOME2Q.WK1 → INCOME2Q.WK1
INCOME3Q.WK1 → INCOME3Q.WK1

A:\ — **Source**   C:\DATA\123DATA — **Target**

This command copies INCOME1Q.WK1, INCOME2Q.WK1 and INCOME3Q.WK1 **from** the root directory of the floppy disk in drive A: (the source), **to** C:\DATA\123DATA (the target), giving them the same names as the original source files.

COPY FILES

COPY TO THE SAME DRIVE

within the same directory

Suppose you want to copy INCOME1Q.WK1 within the same directory and name the new file COPY1Q.WK1.

Note: When copying a file within the same directory, a new filename must be specified.

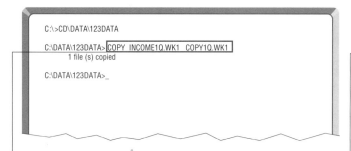

```
C:\>CD\DATA\123DATA

C:\DATA\123DATA> COPY  INCOME1Q.WK1   COPY1Q.WK1
         1 file (s) copied

C:\DATA\123DATA>_
```

1 Change the current directory to where the source file is located (example: type **CD\DATA\123DATA** and press **Enter**).

Note: Since the file is being copied within the same directory, the drive and path can be omitted from the target.

2 To copy **INCOME1Q.WK1**, type:

COPY INCOME1Q.WK1 COPY1Q.WK1

        Source   Target

and press **Enter**.

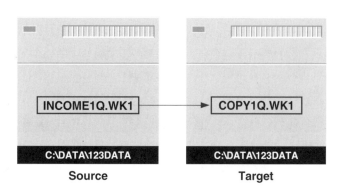

Source   **Target**

This command copies INCOME1Q.WK1 **from** C:\DATA\123DATA (the source), **to** COPY1Q.WK1 in the same directory (the target).

within the same directory using the * (wildcard)

Suppose you want to copy several files (example: NOTE1Q.LET and NOTE2Q.LET) to the same directory, and name them NOTE1Q.NEW and NOTE2Q.NEW.

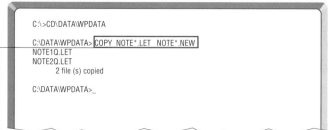

```
C:\>CD\DATA\WPDATA

C:\DATA\WPDATA> COPY  NOTE*.LET   NOTE*.NEW
NOTE1Q.LET
NOTE2Q.LET
         2 file (s) copied

C:\DATA\WPDATA>_
```

1 Change the current directory to where the source file is located (example: type **CD\DATA\WPDATA** and press **Enter**).

Note: Since the file is being copied within the same directory, the drive and path can be omitted from the target.

2 To copy **NOTE1Q.LET** and **NOTE2Q.LET**, type:

COPY NOTE*.LET NOTE*.NEW

        Source   Target

and press **Enter**.

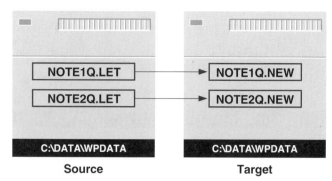

Source   **Target**

This command copies NOTE1Q.LET and NOTE2Q.LET **from** C:\DATA\WPDATA (the source), **to** NOTE1Q.NEW and NOTE2Q.NEW in the same directory (the target).

Using the Command Prompt

Getting Started

Managing Your Directories

Managing Your Files ◄

Managing Your Floppy Disks

Managing Your Hard Disk

to another directory

Suppose you want to copy the file COMMAND.COM from C:\ (the root directory) to C:\DOS.

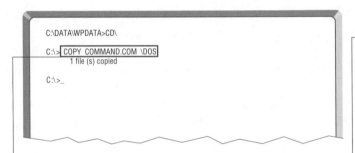

```
C:\DATA\WPDATA>CD\

C:\> COPY COMMAND.COM \DOS
         1 file (s) copied

C:\>_
```

1 Type **CD** and press **Enter** to return to the root directory.

2 To copy **COMMAND.COM**, type:

COPY | COMMAND.COM | \DOS
       Source   Target

and press **Enter**.

Note: The target drive C: is the same as the current drive so, it can be omitted from the target. Also, since the name of the copied file is to be the same on the target, it can also be omitted.

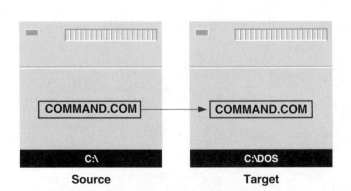

COMMAND.COM	→	COMMAND.COM
C:\		C:\DOS
Source		**Target**

This command copies COMMAND.COM **from** the root directory (the source), **to** COMMAND.COM in the \DOS directory (the target).

---

directly to a disk file

Suppose you want to type a quick memo to yourself of jobs you must do. This feature allows you to create a file from your keyboard, and then save it to your disk drive.

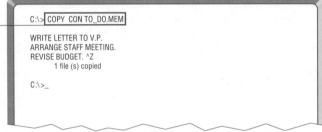

```
C:\> COPY CON TO_DO.MEM

WRITE LETTER TO V.P.
ARRANGE STAFF MEETING.
REVISE BUDGET. ^Z
         1 file (s) copied

C:\>_
```

1 Type **COPY CON TO_DO.MEM** and press **Enter**.

2 Type **WRITE LETTER TO V.P.** Press **Enter**.

Type **ARRANGE STAFF MEETING.** Press **Enter**.

Type **REVISE BUDGET.**

3 Press **F6** or **Ctrl-Z** (displayed on screen as **^Z**). Press **Enter** and the file is copied to the root directory of drive C: and named **TO_DO.MEM**.

Note: **CON** is an abbreviation for **Con**sole (also referred to as Keyboard).

RENAME FILES

The Rename command (typed as REN) allows you to change the name of a file or group of files.

Wildcards (* or ?) can be used in either the filename or extension.

Note: You can only rename files within a directory. Files cannot be renamed across drives or directories.

The Rename command is:		
REN	SOURCE FILE SPECIFICATION	NEW FILENAME AND EXTENSION

SOURCE **FILE SPECIFICATION**	Tells MS-DOS the drive, path, filename and extension of the file to be renamed.
NEW FILENAME **AND EXTENSION**	Tells MS-DOS the new filename and extension.

Note: Always change the current drive and directory to where the file to be renamed is located. The drive and path can then be eliminated from the file specification.

RENAME A FILE

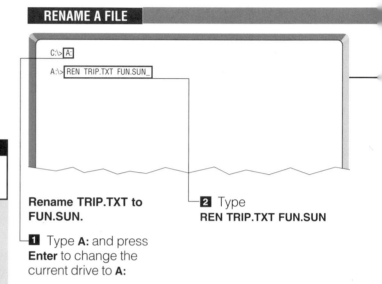

Rename TRIP.TXT to FUN.SUN.

1 Type **A:** and press **Enter** to change the current drive to **A:**

2 Type **REN TRIP.TXT FUN.SUN**

RENAME A FILE USING THE * WILDCARD

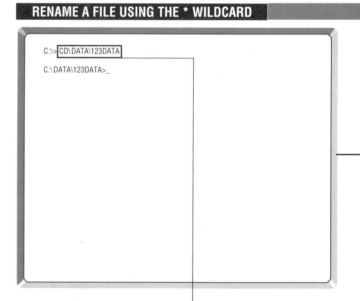

Rename INCOME1Q.WK1 and INCOME2Q.WK1 located in the C:\DATA\123DATA directory to BUDGET1Q.WK1 and BUDGET2Q.WK1.

*Note: Type **C:** and press **Enter** to change the current drive back to **C:***

1 Type **CD\DATA\123DATA** and press **Enter** to change the current directory to **C:\DATA\123DATA**.

```
C:\>A:

A:\>REN TRIP.TXT FUN.SUN

A:\> _
```

3 Press **Enter**. The command prompt **A:\>** appears, indicating the file has been renamed.

*Note: To verify that the file was renamed correctly, type **DIR** and press **Enter** to display the new filename and extension.*

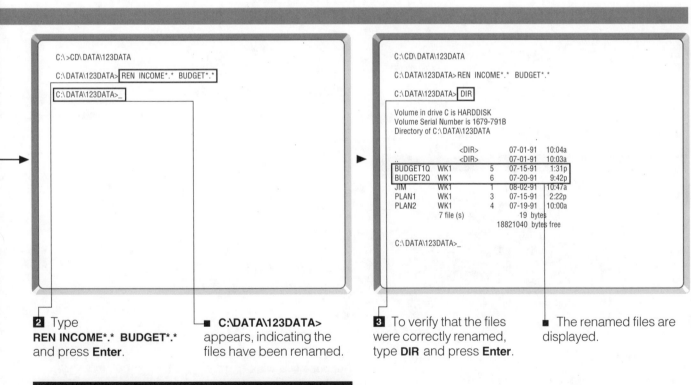

```
C:\>CD\DATA\123DATA

C:\DATA\123DATA> REN INCOME*.*  BUDGET*.*

C:\DATA\123DATA>_
```

```
C:\CD\DATA\123DATA

C:\DATA\123DATA>REN INCOME*.*  BUDGET*.*

C:\DATA\123DATA> DIR

Volume in drive C is HARDDISK
Volume Serial Number is 1679-791B
Directory of C:\DATA\123DATA

.              <DIR>           07-01-91   10:04a
..             <DIR>           07-01-91   10:03a
BUDGET1Q  WK1           5       07-15-91    1:31p
BUDGET2Q  WK1           6       07-20-91    9:42p
JIM       WK1           1       08-02-91   10:47a
PLAN1     WK1           3       07-15-91    2:22p
PLAN2     WK1           4       07-19-91   10:00a
        7 file (s)              19 bytes
                        18821040 bytes free

C:\DATA\123DATA>_
```

2 Type **REN INCOME*.* BUDGET*.*** and press **Enter**.

■ **C:\DATA\123DATA>** appears, indicating the files have been renamed.

3 To verify that the files were correctly renamed, type **DIR** and press **Enter**.

■ The renamed files are displayed.

WARNING
Before renaming files using wildcards (* or ?), first use the DIR command to check if other files will be affected.

Using the Command Prompt

Getting Started

Managing Your Directories

Managing Your Files

Managing Your Floppy Disks

Managing Your Hard Disk

DELETE
FILES

When you save a file, MS-DOS writes the file to the disk and tells a File Allocation Table (FAT) where the file is located on the disk. If a file is deleted, it still remains on the disk, but its connection to the FAT is removed.

To keep track of deleted files, a special Mirror program can be installed to detect the information required to recover deleted files.

The Mirror program is loaded into the computer's active memory or RAM. Therefore, this program must be reinstalled every time you start your computer.

Since Mirror is an external command, the Path command should include C:\DOS. During the installation of MS-DOS 5.0, the Path command C:\DOS is automatically installed in your AUTOEXEC.BAT file.

Note: If for some reason the Path command C:\DOS is not installed in your AUTOEXEC.BAT file, the current drive and directory must be changed to C:\DOS before issuing this command (refer to page 8).

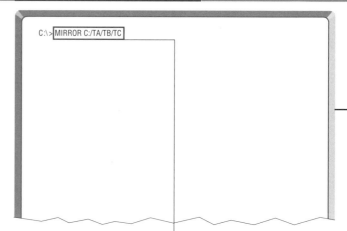

Install the Mirror program to track deleted files on drives A:, B: and C:

1 Type **MIRROR C:/TA/TB/TC** and press **Enter**.

The Delete command (typed as DEL) erases files that are no longer required from your hard or floppy disks.

The Delete command is:

DEL	FILE SPECIFICATION	/P

FILE SPECIFICATION	Tells MS-DOS the drive, path, filename and extension of the files to be deleted.
/P	Tells MS-DOS to request verification before deleting each file.

Note: Always change the current drive and directory to the location of the file to be deleted. The drive and path can then be omitted from the file specification.

The terms "Delete" and "Erase" are used interchangeably.

Suppose you want to delete a file (example: PLAN2.WK1) from the C:\DATA\123DATA directory.

1 Type **DEL PLAN2.WK1**

Note: Make sure you change the current drive and directory to C:\DATA\123DATA before starting Step 1.

Using the Command Prompt

Getting Started

Managing Your Directories

Managing Your Files ◄

Managing Your Floppy Disks

Managing Your Hard Disk

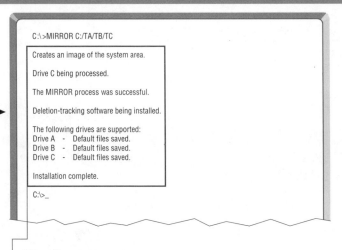

```
C:\>MIRROR C:/TA/TB/TC

Creates an image of the system area.

Drive C being processed.

The MIRROR process was successful.

Deletion-tracking software being installed.

The following drives are supported:
Drive A  -  Default files saved.
Drive B  -  Default files saved.
Drive C  -  Default files saved.

Installation complete.

C:\>_
```

Note: The Mirror program should be loaded each time you start your computer. It is recommended that you include the Mirror command in your AUTOEXEC.BAT file. Refer to the Microsoft MS-DOS 5.0 User's Guide.

Every time you delete a file, the Mirror program records the information required to recover the deleted files in a special deletion-tracking file. The Mirror command C:/TA/TB/TC installs the deletion-tracking software which keeps a running record of files deleted on drives A:, B: and C:

■ The Mirror program, including the deletion-tracking software, has been successfully installed on drives **A:**, **B:** and **C:**

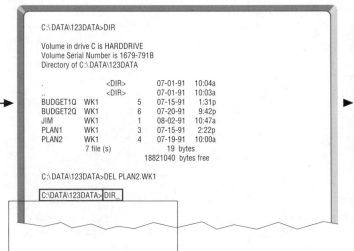

```
C:\DATA\123DATA>DIR

Volume in drive C is HARDDRIVE
Volume Serial Number is 1679-791B
Directory of C:\DATA\123DATA

.              <DIR>         07-01-91   10:04a
..             <DIR>         07-01-91   10:03a
BUDGET1Q   WK1       5       07-15-91    1:31p
BUDGET2Q   WK1       6       07-20-91    9:42p
JIM        WK1       1       08-02-91   10:47a
PLAN1      WK1       3       07-15-91    2:22p
PLAN2      WK1       4       07-19-91   10:00a
          7 file (s)              19 bytes
                          18821040  bytes free

C:\DATA\123DATA>DEL PLAN2.WK1

C:\DATA\123DATA>DIR_
```

```
C:\DATA\123DATA>DIR

Volume in drive C is HARDDRIVE
Volume Serial Number is 1679-791B
Directory of C:\DATA\123DATA

.              <DIR>         07-01-91   10:04a
..             <DIR>         07-01-91   10:03a
BUDGET1Q   WK1       5       07-15-91    1:31p
BUDGET2Q   WK1       6       07-20-91    9:42p
JIM        WK1       1       08-02-91   10:47a
PLAN1      WK1       3       07-15-91    2:22p
          6 file (s)              15 bytes
                          18821044  bytes free

C:\DATA\123DATA>_
```

2 Press **Enter**. The file is erased and a new command prompt appears.

3 To check that the file was deleted, type **DIR** and press **Enter**.

■ This display verifies that **PLAN2.WK1** has been deleted.

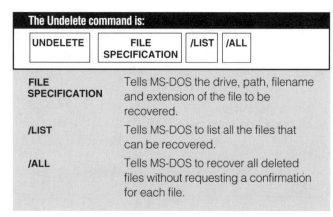

/ DELETE FILES   / UNDELETE FILES

DELETE MULTIPLE FILES USING THE * WILDCARD

C:\DATA\123DATA>`DEL BUDGET*.WK1/P_`

Suppose you want to delete multiple files (example: BUDGET1Q.WK1 and BUDGET2Q.WK1) from C:\DATA\123DATA.

1 Type **DEL BUDGET*.WK1/P** and press **Enter**.

Note: The /P makes MS-DOS request verification before deleting each file.

The Undelete command restores files that were erased using the Delete command. Use the Undelete command immediately after a file is accidentally erased. Do not change or create any new files before using the Undelete command.

Since Undelete is an external command, the Path command should include C:\DOS. During the installation of MS-DOS 5.0, the Path command C:\DOS is automatically installed in your AUTOEXEC.BAT file.

Note: If for some reason the Path command C:\DOS is not installed in your AUTOEXEC.BAT file, the current drive and directory must be changed to C:\DOS before issuing this command (refer to page 8).

LIST ALL DELETED FILES IN THE \DATA\123DATA DIRECTORY

C:\> `CD\DATA\123DATA`

C:\DATA\123DATA> `UNDELETE/LIST`

List all files deleted on pages 38 to 41 (e.g. PLAN2.WK1, BUDGET1Q.WK1 and BUDGET2Q.WK1).

1 Type **CD\DATA\123DATA** and press **Enter** to change the current directory to \DATA\123DATA.

2 Type **UNDELETE/LIST** and press **Enter**.

The Undelete command is:

UNDELETE	FILE SPECIFICATION	/LIST	/ALL

FILE SPECIFICATION	Tells MS-DOS the drive, path, filename and extension of the file to be recovered.
/LIST	Tells MS-DOS to list all the files that can be recovered.
/ALL	Tells MS-DOS to recover all deleted files without requesting a confirmation for each file.

Using the Command Prompt

Getting Started

Managing Your Directories

Managing Your Files

Managing Your Floppy Disks

Managing Your Hard Disk

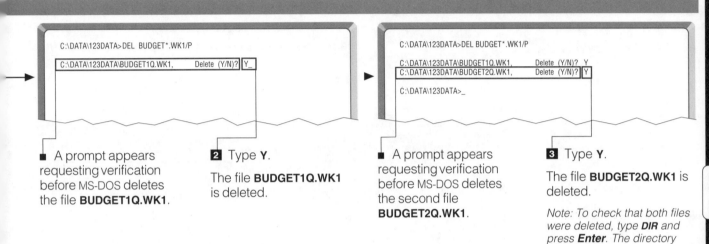

```
C:\DATA\123DATA>DEL BUDGET*.WK1/P

C:\DATA\123DATA\BUDGET1Q.WK1,     Delete (Y/N)? Y_
```

```
C:\DATA\123DATA>DEL BUDGET*.WK1/P

C:\DATA\123DATA\BUDGET1Q.WK1,     Delete (Y/N)?  Y
C:\DATA\123DATA\BUDGET2Q.WK1,     Delete (Y/N)?  Y

C:\DATA\123DATA>_
```

■ A prompt appears requesting verification before MS-DOS deletes the file **BUDGET1Q.WK1**.

2 Type **Y**.

The file **BUDGET1Q.WK1** is deleted.

■ A prompt appears requesting verification before MS-DOS deletes the second file **BUDGET2Q.WK1**.

3 Type **Y**.

The file **BUDGET2Q.WK1** is deleted.

Note: To check that both files were deleted, type DIR and press Enter. The directory display will not include the BUDGET1Q.WK1 and BUDGET2Q.WK1 files.

IMPORTANT

If you accidentally delete a file or group of files, you may still be able to recover them with the Undelete command described on page 40.

Do not perform any other MS-DOS operations until you use the Undelete command.

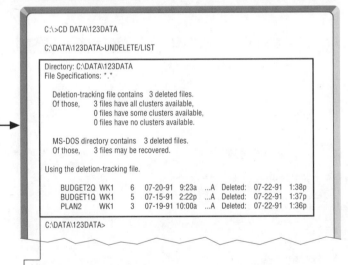

```
C:\>CD DATA\123DATA

C:\DATA\123DATA>UNDELETE/LIST

Directory: C:\DATA\123DATA
File Specifications: *.*

    Deletion-tracking file contains  3 deleted files.
    Of those,   3 files have all clusters available,
                0 files have some clusters available,
                0 files have no clusters available.

    MS-DOS directory contains  3 deleted files.
    Of those,   3 files may be recovered.

Using the deletion-tracking file.

    BUDGET2Q  WK1    6   07-20-91  9:23a  ...A  Deleted:  07-22-91  1:38p
    BUDGET1Q  WK1    5   07-15-91  2:22p  ...A  Deleted:  07-22-91  1:37p
    PLAN2     WK1    3   07-19-91 10:00a  ...A  Deleted:  07-22-91  1:36p

C:\DATA\123DATA>
```

■ MS-DOS lists all deleted files in the **C:\DATA\123DATA** directory that can be recovered.

Note: The Undelete command applies to files erased from the current directory.

To undelete files in another drive/directory from the current directory, you must type their complete file specification (example: Undelete C:\DOS*.BAK/LIST).

UNDELETE FILES

UNDELETE AN ERASED FILE IN THE CURRENT DIRECTORY

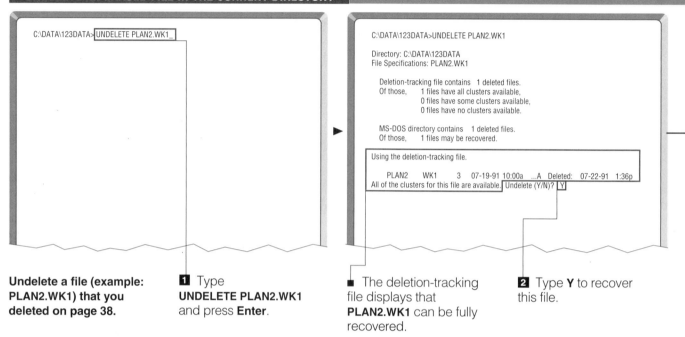

```
C:\DATA\123DATA>UNDELETE PLAN2.WK1_
```

Undelete a file (example: PLAN2.WK1) that you deleted on page 38.

1 Type **UNDELETE PLAN2.WK1** and press **Enter**.

```
C:\DATA\123DATA>UNDELETE PLAN2.WK1

Directory: C:\DATA\123DATA
File Specifications: PLAN2.WK1

    Deletion-tracking file contains   1 deleted files.
    Of those,      1 files have all clusters available,
                   0 files have some clusters available,
                   0 files have no clusters available.

    MS-DOS directory contains   1 deleted files.
    Of those,      1 files may be recovered.

Using the deletion-tracking file.

    PLAN2     WK1     3   07-19-91  10:00a  ...A  Deleted:  07-22-91  1:36p
All of the clusters for this file are available. Undelete (Y/N)? Y
```

■ The deletion-tracking file displays that **PLAN2.WK1** can be fully recovered.

2 Type **Y** to recover this file.

UNDELETE ALL ERASED FILES IN THE CURRENT DIRECTORY

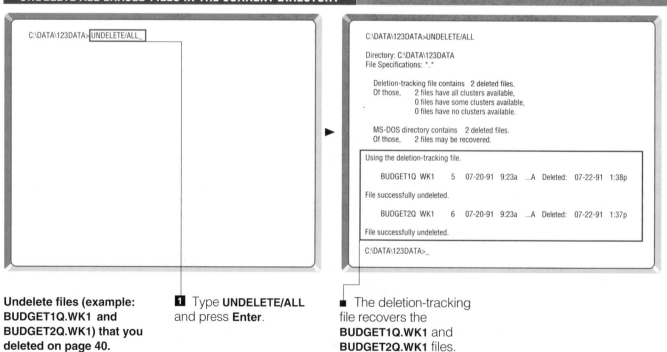

```
C:\DATA\123DATA>UNDELETE/ALL_
```

Undelete files (example: BUDGET1Q.WK1 and BUDGET2Q.WK1) that you deleted on page 40.

1 Type **UNDELETE/ALL** and press **Enter**.

```
C:\DATA\123DATA>UNDELETE/ALL

Directory: C:\DATA\123DATA
File Specifications: *.*

    Deletion-tracking file contains   2 deleted files.
    Of those,      2 files have all clusters available,
                   0 files have some clusters available,
                   0 files have no clusters available.

    MS-DOS directory contains   2 deleted files.
    Of those,      2 files may be recovered.

Using the deletion-tracking file.

    BUDGET1Q  WK1     5   07-20-91  9:23a  ...A  Deleted:  07-22-91  1:38p

File successfully undeleted.

    BUDGET2Q  WK1     6   07-20-91  9:23a  ...A  Deleted:  07-22-91  1:37p

File successfully undeleted.

C:\DATA\123DATA>_
```

■ The deletion-tracking file recovers the **BUDGET1Q.WK1** and **BUDGET2Q.WK1** files.

```
C:\DATA\123DATA>UNDELETE PLAN2.WK1

Directory: C:\DATA\123DATA
File Specifications: PLAN2.WK1

    Deletion-tracking file contains   1 deleted files.
    Of those,      1 files have all clusters available,
                   0 files have some clusters available,
                   0 files have no clusters available.

    MS-DOS directory contains    1 deleted files.
    Of those,      1 files may be recovered.

Using the deletion-tracking file.

    PLAN2     WK1      3    07-19-91  10:00a   ...A  Deleted:   07-22-91   1:36p
All of the clusters for this file are available.  Undelete (Y/N)? Y

┌──────────────────────────┐
│ File successfully undeleted. │
└──────────────────────────┘

C:\DATA\123DATA>_
```

Note: If the deletion-tracking program is not present, Undelete can still recover files using the MS-DOS directory method. It does this by substituting a number sign (#) for the missing first character in the filename (which is removed when a file is deleted). You are then asked to supply the missing character.

However, if the deletion-tracking program is present, it detects and saves the missing character and replaces it during the Undelete process. Deletion-tracking is more reliable than using the MS-DOS directory method listing of deleted files.

If the deletion-tracking file is present, it always supersedes the MS-DOS directory method of undeleting files.

■ The screen displays that the file was successfully undeleted.

*Note: Type **DIR** and press **Enter** to confirm that **PLAN2.WK1** was successfully recovered.*

Note: If the deletion-tracking file is not present, Undelete/All can still recover files using the MS-DOS directory method. It does this by supplying a number sign (#) for the missing first character in the recovered filenames. You are then asked to supply the correct first letter of the filename before the file can be undeleted.

Using the
Command
Prompt

Getting
Started

Managing
Your
Directories

**Managing
Your
Files**

Managing
Your
Floppy Disks

Managing
Your
Hard Disk

TYPE FILES   PRINT FILES

TYPE

The Type command displays the contents of a file on your computer screen. It will work on most files containing text.

Note: If you try to type an MS-DOS or application program file, the screen will be filled with machine code symbols.

The Type command is:

TYPE	FILE SPECIFICATION

FILE SPECIFICATION	Tells MS-DOS the drive, path, filename and extension of the file you want to display on screen.

Note: Always change the current drive and directory to where the file you want to display is located. The drive and path can then be omitted from the file specification.

```
C:\> TYPE TO_DO.MEM_
```

Display a text file (example: TO_DO.MEM located in the C:\ (root directory)) on the screen.

Note: The TO_DO.MEM file was created on page 35.

1 Type **TYPE TO_DO.MEM** and press **Enter**.

*Note: If the **TO_DO.MEM** file contains more than one screen of text, type* **TO_DO.MEM¦MORE** *and press* **Enter**. *One screen of text is displayed. Press any key to display the next screen of text.*

PRINT

The Print command allows you to print the contents of any text file.

Since Print is an external command, the Path command should include C:\DOS. During the installation of MS-DOS 5.0, the Path command C:\DOS is automatically installed in your AUTOEXEC.BAT file.

Note: If for some reason the Path command C:\DOS is not installed in your AUTOEXEC.BAT file, the current drive and directory must be changed to C:\DOS before issuing this command (refer to page 8).

The Print command is:

PRINT	FILE SPECIFICATION

FILE SPECIFICATION	Tells MS-DOS the drive, path, filename and extension of the file you want to print.

```
C:\ > PRINT \DATA\WPDATA\MEMO.1
C:\DATA\WPDATA\MEMO.1 is currently being printed
C:\>_
```

Print a text file named MEMO.1 located in the C:\DATA\WPDATA subdirectory.

1 Type **PRINT \DATA\WPDATA\MEMO.1** and press **Enter**.

2 MS-DOS displays a message that the file **MEMO.1** is being printed.

Note: If MEMO.1 is located in the root directory of the floppy disk in drive A:, type **PRINT A:\MEMO.1** *and press* **Enter**.

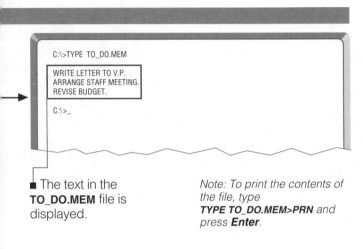

■ The text in the **TO_DO.MEM** file is displayed.

*Note: To print the contents of the file, type **TYPE TO_DO.MEM>PRN** and press **Enter**.*

PRINT SCREEN

To print the entire screen, press [Print Screen] or [Shift] [PrtSc]. Make sure your printer is connected and turned on.

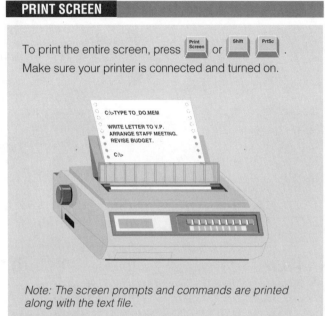

Note: The screen prompts and commands are printed along with the text file.

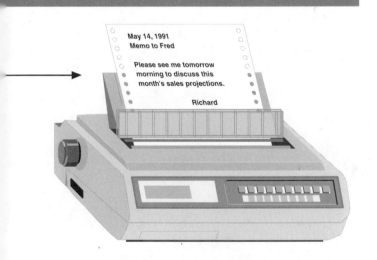

Using the Command Prompt

Getting Started

Managing Your Directories

Managing Your Files ◀

Managing Your Floppy Disks

Managing Your Hard Disk

3.5" AND 5.25" FLOPPY DISKS

The MS-DOS commands in this chapter work on entire floppy disks instead of individual files.

The first IBM microcomputers used 5.25 inch floppy disks with only 160K of memory capacity. As the technology improved, double-sided high capacity floppy disks became available with 1200K (or 1.2MB) of memory.

With the release of the IBM PS/2 family of microcomputers, 3.5 inch high capacity, 720K and 1.44MB floppy disks were added to the line.

MS-DOS 5.0 supports high capacity floppy drives that can format floppy disks to 2.88MB.

Note: K is an abbreviation for Kilobytes (1,024 bytes). A byte represents one character.

MB is an abbreviation for Megabytes (1,048,576 bytes).

FLOPPY DISK SIZES AND CAPACITY

Size	Capacity	Standard Hardware	DOS Versions
5.25 inch	1.2MB	IBM AT or compatibles	Version 3 or later
5.25 inch	360K	IBM PC, PC/XT or compatibles	Version 2 or later
5.25 inch	320K	IBM PC, PC/XT or compatibles	All Versions
5.25 inch	180K	IBM PC, PC/XT or compatibles	Version 2 or later
5.25 inch	160K	IBM PC, PC/XT or compatibles	All Versions
3.5 inch	2.88MB	IBM PS/2	Version 5.0 (If the hardware contains a 2.88MB floppy drive)
3.5 inch	1.44MB	IBM PS/2, PC/AT or compatibles	Version 3.3 or later
3.5 inch	720K	IBM PS/2 Model 30 and compatibles	Version 3.2 or later

5.25 INCH FLOPPY DISK

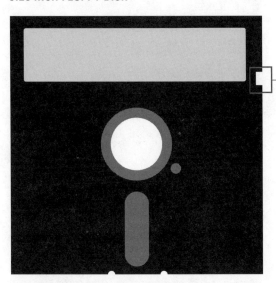

WRITE PROTECT NOTCH

The open notch on the right side of the floppy disk lets you copy information to or delete information from the disk.

By placing a small piece of tape over the notch, the floppy disk becomes write protected. You can still use the disk, but you cannot add or delete information to or from it.

Floppy disks that do not have a notch are permanently write protected. Many application programs are permanently write protected to guard their files from being deleted or modified.

3.5 INCH FLOPPY DISK

WRITE PROTECT SWITCH

The switch works similar to the notch on the 5.25 inch floppy disk. With the switch in the closed position, you can erase, modify or add information to the floppy disk.

With the switch in the open position, as illustrated to the left, the disk is write protected.

Note: Make sure your floppy disks are properly labeled and protected from extreme heat or cold, humidity, food and drinks.

Keep floppy disks away from magnetic influences such as telephones, magnetic paper clip holders, or the computer monitor.

Using the Command Prompt

Getting Started

Managing Your Directories

Managing Your Files

Managing Your Floppy Disks

Managing Your Hard Disk

FORMAT

The Format command prepares a blank or previously formatted floppy disk for data and program file storage. This command checks for bad sectors on the floppy disk, and sets up a File Allocation Table (to track the location of each file on the disk). It also creates a root directory (to store the name, extension, size, creation date and time of all files on the disk).

Since Format is an external command, the Path command should include C:\DOS. During the installation of MS-DOS 5.0, the Path command C:\DOS is automatically installed in your AUTOEXEC.BAT file.

Note: If for some reason the Path command C:\DOS is not installed in your AUTOEXEC.BAT file, the current drive and directory must be changed to C:\DOS before issuing this command (refer to page 8).

The Format command is:

FORMAT	DRIVE

DRIVE	Tells MS-DOS the drive that contains the floppy disk you want to format (A: or B:).

Caution

Do not format a floppy disk containing information you want to retain.

If you accidentally format a floppy disk, it may be possible to recover all the files on the disk using the Unformat command. Refer to the Microsoft User's Guide or check with a system specialist.

FORMAT A FLOPPY DISK AND GIVE IT A VOLUME LABEL

```
C:\> FORMAT B:
Insert new diskette for drive B:
and press ENTER when ready...

Checking existing disk format
Saving UNFORMAT information
Verifying 1.44M
 xx percent of disk formatted
```

Format a floppy disk in drive A: or B: and give it a Volume label (example: MEMOS).

1 Type **FORMAT B:**

Note: MS-DOS automatically formats a disk to the maximum capacity of the drive. To format a floppy disk to lower capacities, refer to the F:<size> switch on page 50.

2 Press **Enter** and the prompt above appears.

3 Insert the floppy disk you want formatted into drive B: and press **Enter**.

■ MS-DOS reports its progress with the message "xx percent of disk formatted".

Caution

Do not format the C: drive unless you have checked with a system specialist.

ADD SYSTEM STARTUP FILES TO FLOPPY DISK

To add the system startup files while formatting a floppy disk, type **FORMAT A:/S** or **FORMAT B:/S**. You can then start MS-DOS directly from the floppy disk. Adding the **/S** option reduces the storage capacity of the floppy disk by approximately 120K.

Using the
Command
Prompt

Getting
Started

Managing
Your
Directories

Managing
Your
Files

Managing
Your
Floppy Disks

Managing
Your
Hard Disk

```
C:\>FORMAT B:
Insert new diskette for drive B:
and press ENTER when ready...

Checking existing disk format
Saving UNFORMAT information
Verifying 1.44M
Format complete

Volume label (11 characters, ENTER for none)? MEMOS_
```

```
C:\>FORMAT B:
Insert new diskette for drive B:
and press ENTER when ready...

Checking existing disk format
Saving UNFORMAT information
Verifying 1.44M
Format complete

Volume label (11 characters, ENTER for none)? MEMOS

     1457664   bytes total disk space
       53760   bytes in bad sectors
     1403904   bytes available on disk

         512   bytes in each allocation unit
        2847   allocation units available on disk

Volume Serial Number is 1353-10F6

Format another (Y/N) ?_
```

■ The above message
appears when the floppy
disk is formatted.

4 Type a Volume label
(example: **MEMOS**) and
press **Enter**. If no Volume
label is required, just
press **Enter**.

*Note: The label can contain
up to 11 characters including
one blank space. Permissible
characters are the letters A
to Z, digits 0 through 9, and
$ – ( ) _ { } #.*

■ MS-DOS then tells you
the total capacity of the
floppy disk, unusable
bytes in bad sectors, and
bytes for storing new data.

*Note: Do not use a floppy
disk with bad sectors. This
floppy disk has bad sectors
and should not be used. If
the disk is OK, the "bytes in
bad sectors" line will not
appear.*

5 MS-DOS asks you if
you want to format
another floppy disk:

– Type **Y** and press
  Enter to format
  another disk.

        or

– Type **N** and press
  Enter to return to the
  system prompt.

TO VIEW THE VOLUME LABEL

```
B:\> VOL

Volume in drive B is MEMOS
Volume Serial number is 1353-10F6
```

1 Type **VOL** and press
Enter.

*Note: Type **B:** and press
Enter to change the current
drive to **B:***

■ The Volume label is
used to quickly identify
the name of the disk
(hard or floppy).

FORMAT

```
C:\>FORMAT A:/F:360
```

```
C:\>FORMAT A:/F:360
Insert new diskette for drive A:
and press ENTER when ready...

Checking existing disk format
Existing format differs from that specified
This disk cannot be unformatted
Proceed with Format (Y/N)? Y
Formatting 360K
  xx percent of disk formatted
```

▶

The F:<size> switch permits you to format a 3.5 or 5.25 inch floppy disk to a lower capacity than the drive supports.

This is very useful when you are sharing information with machines having lower capacity drives.

Format a floppy disk (example: 5.25 inch disk to 360K).

1 Type **FORMAT A:/F:360**

Note: Do not format a floppy disk to a size greater than its guaranteed capacity.

If you format a 360K floppy disk in a high capacity drive, it can be used in that drive. Due to hardware differences, some lower capacity drives are unable to reliably read disks formatted on a higher capacity drive using the F:<size>switch.

2 Press **Enter** and the above prompt appears.

3 Insert the floppy disk you want to format in drive A: and press **Enter**.

■ The above prompt appears. It means the floppy disk was previously formatted at another capacity, probably 1.2M.

4 Type **Y** and press **Enter** to start the floppy disk formatting process.

Floppy Disk Size	Floppy Disk Capacity	F:<size>
5.25"	160K	160
5.25"	180K	180
5.25"	320K	320
5.25"	360K	360
3.5"	720K	720
3.5"	1.44MB	1440

Using the
Command
Prompt

Getting
Started

Managing
Your
Directories

Managing
Your
Files

Managing
Your
Floppy Disks

Managing
Your
Hard Disk

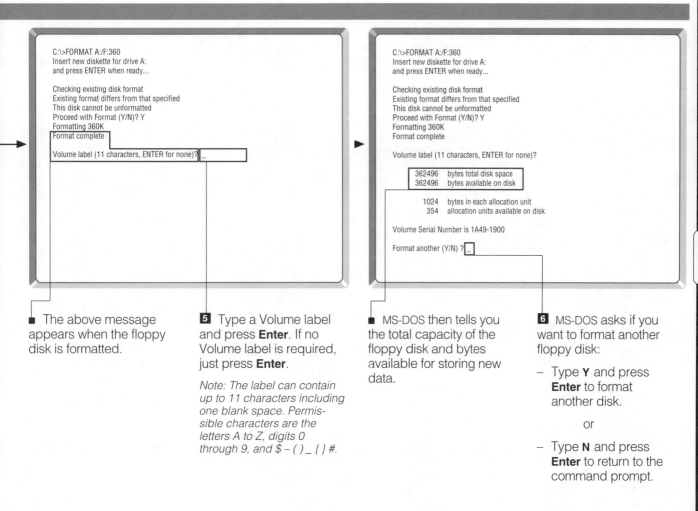

```
C:\>FORMAT A:/F:360
Insert new diskette for drive A:
and press ENTER when ready...

Checking existing disk format
Existing format differs from that specified
This disk cannot be unformatted
Proceed with Format (Y/N)? Y
Formatting 360K
Format complete

Volume label (11 characters, ENTER for none)? _
```

```
C:\>FORMAT A:/F:360
Insert new diskette for drive A:
and press ENTER when ready...

Checking existing disk format
Existing format differs from that specified
This disk cannot be unformatted
Proceed with Format (Y/N)? Y
Formatting 360K
Format complete

Volume label (11 characters, ENTER for none)?

    362496    bytes total disk space
    362496    bytes available on disk

      1024    bytes in each allocation unit
       354    allocation units available on disk

Volume Serial Number is 1A49-1900

Format another (Y/N) ? _
```

■ The above message appears when the floppy disk is formatted.

5 Type a Volume label and press **Enter**. If no Volume label is required, just press **Enter**.

Note: The label can contain up to 11 characters including one blank space. Permissible characters are the letters A to Z, digits 0 through 9, and $ – ( ) _ { } #.

■ MS-DOS then tells you the total capacity of the floppy disk and bytes available for storing new data.

6 MS-DOS asks if you want to format another floppy disk:

– Type **Y** and press **Enter** to format another disk.

or

– Type **N** and press **Enter** to return to the command prompt.

FORMAT A HARD DRIVE

Formatting a hard drive is an advanced topic. If you accidentally format a hard drive containing valuable programs and data files, you may still be able to recover these files with the Unformat command. Refer to the Microsoft User's Guide or check with a system specialist.

DISKCOPY

The Diskcopy command is used to copy the entire contents of one floppy disk to another floppy disk, so that the second disk is an exact copy of the first.

Since Diskcopy makes an identical copy of the source to the target floppy disk, fragmented files on the source disk are transferred to the target disk.

Note: Fragmented files are created as a disk fills ups. The computer breaks up (or fragments) files into allocation units and stores them in different areas of the disk. Fragmented files take longer to access and save.

Since Diskcopy is an external command, the Path command should include C:\DOS. During the installation of MS-DOS 5.0, the Path command C:\DOS is automatically installed in your AUTOEXEC.BAT file.

Note: If for some reason the Path command C:\DOS is not installed in your AUTOEXEC.BAT file, the current drive and directory must be changed to C:\DOS before issuing this command (refer to page 8).

The Diskcopy command is:		
DISKCOPY	SOURCE DRIVE	TARGET DRIVE

SOURCE DRIVE	Tells MS-DOS the drive the files are copied **from**.
TARGET DRIVE	Tells MS-DOS the drive the files are copied **to**.

Caution
The Diskcopy command automatically formats the target floppy disk during the copy process, destroying its existing contents. Make sure the target floppy disk does not contain any files that you want to keep.

DISKCOPY USING ONE DRIVE

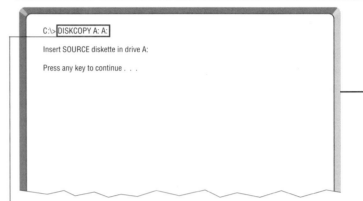

C:\> DISKCOPY A: A:

Insert SOURCE diskette in drive A:

Press any key to continue . . .

1 Type **DISKCOPY A: A:** and press **Enter**.

*Note: Make sure a blank space is left between **A: A:** as you type it.*

2 Insert the **SOURCE** floppy disk into drive A: and press any key.

DISKCOPY USING TWO DRIVES

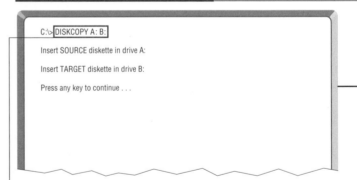

C:\> DISKCOPY A: B:

Insert SOURCE diskette in drive A:

Insert TARGET diskette in drive B:

Press any key to continue . . .

1 Type **DISKCOPY A: B:** and press **Enter**.

2 Insert the **SOURCE** floppy disk in drive A: and the **TARGET** floppy disk in drive B: and press any key.

Note: This only works on floppy disks of the same size and capacity.

Using the
Command
Prompt

Getting
Started

Managing
Your
Directories

Managing
Your
Files

Managing
Your
Floppy Disks

Managing
Your
Hard Disk

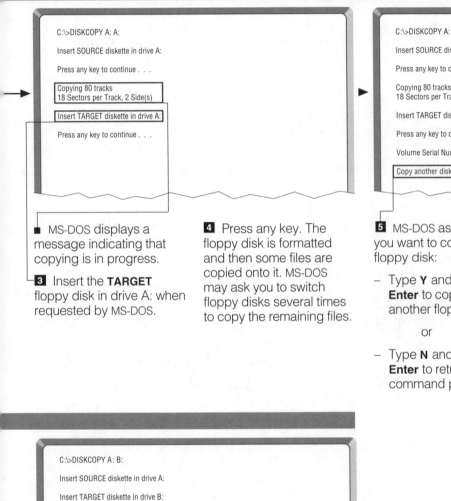

```
C:\>DISKCOPY A: A:

Insert SOURCE diskette in drive A:

Press any key to continue . . .

Copying 80 tracks
18 Sectors per Track, 2 Side(s)

Insert TARGET diskette in drive A:

Press any key to continue . . .
```

```
C:\>DISKCOPY A: A:

Insert SOURCE diskette in drive A:

Press any key to continue . . .

Copying 80 tracks
18 Sectors per Track, 2 Side(s)

Insert TARGET diskette in drive A:

Press any key to continue . . .

Volume Serial Number is 1FF5-1752

Copy another diskette (Y/N)? _
```

■ MS-DOS displays a
message indicating that
copying is in progress.

3 Insert the **TARGET**
floppy disk in drive A: when
requested by MS-DOS.

4 Press any key. The
floppy disk is formatted
and then some files are
copied onto it. MS-DOS
may ask you to switch
floppy disks several times
to copy the remaining files.

5 MS-DOS asks you if
you want to copy another
floppy disk:

– Type **Y** and press
Enter to copy
another floppy disk.

        or

– Type **N** and press
Enter to return to the
command prompt.

```
C:\>DISKCOPY A: B:

Insert SOURCE diskette in drive A:

Insert TARGET diskette in drive B:

Press any key when to continue . . .

Copying 80 tracks
18 Sectors per Track, 2 Side(s)

Volume Serial Number is 1FF9-2D2B

Copy another diskette (Y/N)? _
```

■ MS-DOS displays a
message indicating that
copying is in progress.

3 MS-DOS asks you if you
want to copy another
floppy disk:

– Type **Y** and press
Enter to copy
another floppy disk.

        or

– Type **N** and press
Enter to return to the
command prompt.

BACKUP

The Backup command copies data files on your hard disk to backup floppy disk(s). This protects your data in case of a catastrophic failure of your hard disk or accidental erasure of important files.

Backup your data files regularly (daily or weekly).

The complete Backup procedure consists of two commands—Backup and Restore. The Backup command is described on these two pages. The Restore command is described on the next two pages.

Since Backup is an external command, the Path command should include C:\DOS. During the installation of MS-DOS 5.0, the Path command C:\DOS is automatically installed in your AUTOEXEC.BAT file.

Note: If for some reason the Path command C:\DOS is not installed in your AUTOEXEC.BAT file, the current drive and directory must be changed to C:\DOS before issuing this command (refer to page 8).

The Backup command is:

BACKUP	SOURCE FILE SPECIFICATION	TARGET DRIVE	/S	/F

SOURCE FILE SPECIFICATION	Tells MS-DOS the drive, path, filenames and extensions of the files to be backed up.
TARGET DRIVE	Tells MS-DOS the drive the files are to be backed up to.
/S	Tells MS-DOS to backup files in all subdirectories below the directory specified in the source file specification.
/F	Tells MS-DOS to format the target floppy disk if it is not already formatted.

*Note: If you do not specify a filename and extension, MS-DOS uses *.* as the default filename and extension.*

Backup all files and directories starting from the \DATA directory to a series of floppy disks. The number of disks required depends on the total size of the files to be backed up and the size of the disks used.

Backup floppy disks required

To backup **5,500K** of data files with **720K** floppy disks requires **5,500 ÷ 720 = 8** disks.

Note: Since you already have the original application programs and MS-DOS floppy disks, these files are not normally backed up using this command.

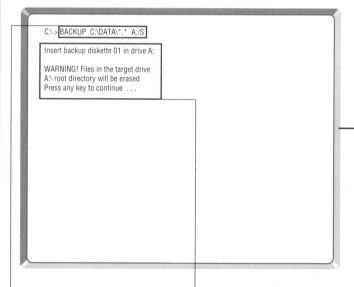

1 Type
BACKUP C:\DATA*.* A:/S
and press **Enter**.

Note: If \DATA is not specified, MS-DOS backs up files from the current directory (C:\ in this example).

2 Insert Backup floppy disk **01** in drive **A:** and press any key.

Using the
Command
Prompt

Getting
Started

Managing
Your
Directories

Managing
Your
Files

Managing
Your
Floppy Disks

Managing
Your
Hard Disk

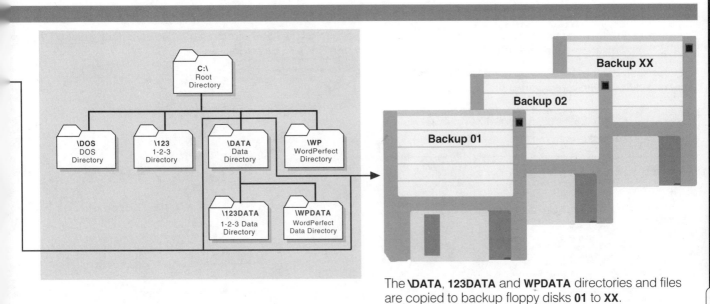

The **\DATA**, **123DATA** and **WPDATA** directories and files are copied to backup floppy disks **01** to **XX**.

```
C:\>BACKUP  C:\DATA\*.*  A:/S

Insert backup diskette 01 in drive A:

WARNING! Files in the target drive
A:\ root directory will be erased
Press any key to continue . . .

*** Backing up files to drive A:  ***
Diskette Number: 01

\DATA\123DATA\INCOME1Q.WK1
\DATA\123DATA\INCOME2Q.WK1
\DATA\123DATA\JIM.WK1
\DATA\123DATA\PLAN1Q.WK1
\DATA\123DATA\PLAN2Q.WK1
\DATA\123DATA\PLAN3Q.WK1
\DATA\123DATA\PLAN4Q.WK1
\DATA\123DATA\PROJECT1.WK1
\DATA\123DATA\PROJECT2.WK1
\DATA\123DATA\PROJECT3.WK1
\DATA\123DATA\PROJECT4.WK1
\DATA\123DATA\PROJECT5.WK1
```

```
Insert backup diskette 02 in drive A:

WARNING! Files in the target dirve
A:\ root directory will be erased
Press any key to continue . . .

*** Backing up files to drive A: ***
Diskette Number: 02

\DATA\WPDATA\SALES4Q.WK1
\DATA\WPDATA\1QPROFIT.MEM
\DATA\WPDATA\2QPROFIT.MEM
\DATA\WPDATA\3QPROFIT.MEM
\DATA\WPDATA\A_FILE.WRI
\DATA\WPDATA\DO-MON.TXT
\DATA\WPDATA\DO-TUES.TXT
\DATA\WPDATA\DO-WED.TXT
\DATA\WPDATA\MERGE.LET
\DATA\WPDATA\NOTE1Q.LET
\DATA\WPDATA\NOTE2Q.LET

C:\>_
```

■ MS-DOS begins backing up files to floppy disk **01** in drive **A:**.

3 Remove Backup floppy disk **01**. Insert Backup floppy disk **02** in drive **A:** and press any key.

■ The remaining files are backed up to floppy disk **02** in drive **A:**. When the **C:** prompt appears, all files are backed up.

Note: More than two backup floppy disks may be required.

◀ 55

RESTORE

The Restore command is used to restore data files on backup floppy disks to your hard drive.

Files duplicated using the Backup command can only be accessed with the Restore command.

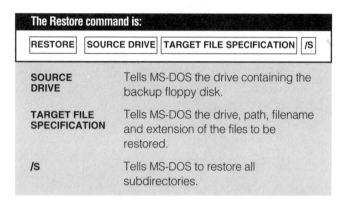

The Restore command is:

| RESTORE | SOURCE DRIVE | TARGET FILE SPECIFICATION | /S |

SOURCE DRIVE	Tells MS-DOS the drive containing the backup floppy disk.
TARGET FILE SPECIFICATION	Tells MS-DOS the drive, path, filename and extension of the files to be restored.
/S	Tells MS-DOS to restore all subdirectories.

RESTORE ALL FILES AND DIRECTORIES

Restore all files and directories on backup floppy disks to the C:\DATA directory.

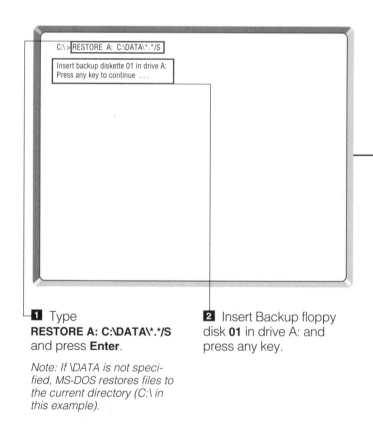

```
C:\>RESTORE A: C:\DATA\*.*/S

Insert backup diskette 01 in drive A:
Press any key to continue . . .
```

1 Type
RESTORE A: C:\DATA*.*/S
and press **Enter**.

Note: If \DATA is not specified, MS-DOS restores files to the current directory (C:\ in this example).

2 Insert Backup floppy disk **01** in drive A: and press any key.

Using the
Command
Prompt

Getting
Started

Managing
Your
Directories

Managing
Your
Files

Managing
Your
Floppy Disks

Managing
Your
Hard Disk

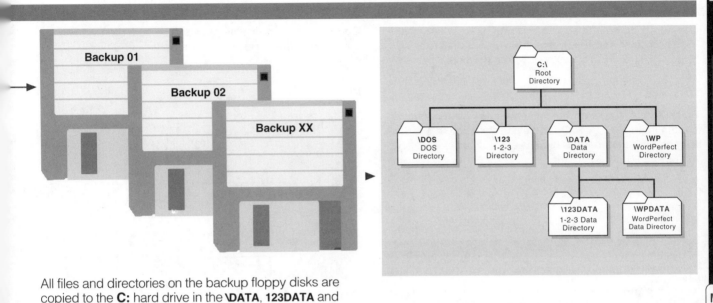

All files and directories on the backup floppy disks are copied to the **C:** hard drive in the **\DATA**, **123DATA** and **WPDATA** directories.

```
C:\>RESTORE A: C:\DATA\*.*/S

Insert backup diskette 01 in drive A:
Press any key to continue . . .

*** Files were backed up 05-28-91 ***

*** Restoring files from drive A: ***
Diskette Number: 01
\DATA\123DATA\INCOME1Q.WK1
\DATA\123DATA\INCOME2Q.WK1
\DATA\123DATA\JIM.WK1
\DATA\123DATA\PLAN1Q.WK1
\DATA\123DATA\PLAN2Q.WK1
\DATA\123DATA\PLAN3Q.WK1
\DATA\123DATA\PLAN4Q.WK1
\DATA\123DATA\PROJECT1.WK1
\DATA\123DATA\PROJECT2.WK1
\DATA\123DATA\PROJECT3.WK1
\DATA\123DATA\PROJECT4.WK1
\DATA\123DATA\PROJECT5.WK1
```

```
Insert backup diskette 02 in drive A:
Press any key to continue . . .

*** Restoring files from drive A: ***
Diskette: 02
\DATA\WPDATA\SALES4Q.WK1
\DATA\WPDATA\1QPROFIT.MEM
\DATA\WPDATA\2QPROFIT.MEM
\DATA\WPDATA\3QPROFIT.MEM
\DATA\WPDATA\A_FILE.WRI
\DATA\WPDATA\DO-MON.TXT
\DATA\WPDATA\DO-TUES.TXT
\DATA\WPDATA\DO-WED.TXT
\DATA\WPDATA\MERGE.LET
\DATA\WPDATA\NOTE1Q.LET
\DATA\WPDATA\NOTE2Q.LET

C:\>_
```

■ MS-DOS begins restoring files to the hard drive **\DATA** directory.

3 Remove Backup floppy disk **01**. Insert Backup floppy disk **02** in drive A: and press any key.

■ Continue following the prompts until the remaining files are restored.

XCOPY

The Xcopy command copies files and directories, including lower level subdirectories, from a hard disk to a floppy disk, or from a floppy disk to a hard disk.

Note: The Copy command can only copy files. It cannot copy directories.

Since Xcopy is an external command, the Path command should include C:\DOS. During the installation of MS-DOS 5.0, the Path command C:\DOS is automatically installed in your AUTOEXEC.BAT file.

Note: If for some reason the Path command C:\DOS is not installed in your AUTOEXEC.BAT file, the current drive and directory must be changed to C:\DOS before issuing this command (refer to page 8).

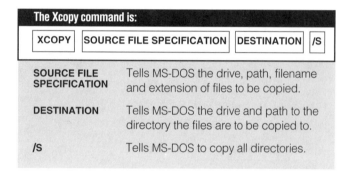

The Xcopy command is:			
XCOPY	SOURCE FILE SPECIFICATION	DESTINATION	/S

SOURCE FILE SPECIFICATION	Tells MS-DOS the drive, path, filename and extension of files to be copied.
DESTINATION	Tells MS-DOS the drive and path to the directory the files are to be copied to.
/S	Tells MS-DOS to copy all directories.

*Note: If you do not specify a filename and extension, XCOPY uses *.* as the default filename and extension.*

Copy all files and directories starting from the C:\DATA directory to the floppy disk in drive A:

Then copy the files from the floppy disk in drive A: back to hard drive C:

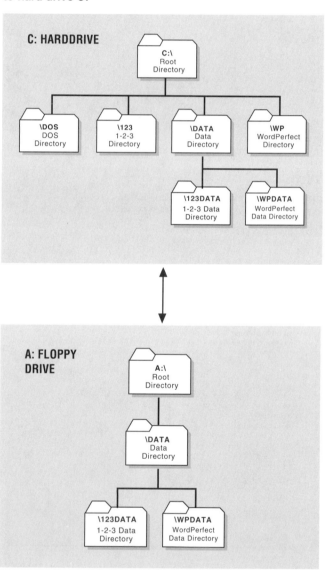

Note: XCOPY should only be used when the size of the files copied are less than the capacity of one floppy disk.

Using the
Command
Prompt

Getting
Started

Managing
Your
Directories

Managing
Your
Files

Managing
Your
Floppy Disks

Managing
Your
Hard Disk

COPY FILES AND DIRECTORIES FROM A HARD DISK TO A FLOPPY DISK

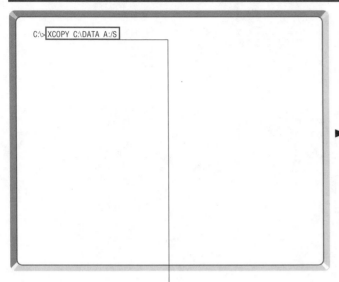

```
C:\> XCOPY C:\DATA A:/S
```

```
Reading source file(s)...
C:\DATA\123DATA\INCOME1Q.WK1
C:\DATA\123DATA\INCOME2Q.WK1
C:\DATA\123DATA\INCOME3Q.WK1
C:\DATA\123DATA\JIM.WK1
C:\DATA\123DATA\PLAN1.WK1
C:\DATA\123DATA\PLAN2.WK1
C:\DATA\123DATA\PLAN3.WK1
C:\DATA\123DATA\PROJECT1.WK1
C:\DATA\123DATA\PROJECT2.WK1
C:\DATA\123DATA\PROJECT3.WK1
C:\DATA\WPDATA\1QPROFIT.MEM
C:\DATA\WPDATA\2QPROFIT.MEM
C:\DATA\WPDATA\3QPROFIT.MEM
C:\DATA\WPDATA\DO_MON.LET
C:\DATA\WPDATA\DO_TUES.LET
C:\DATA\WPDATA\MERGE.LET
C:\DATA\WPDATA\NOTE1Q.TXT
C:\DATA\WPDATA\NOTE2Q.TXT
C:\DATA\WPDATA\TEST.LET
C:\DATA\WPDATA\TRAINING.LET
       20 File(s) copied
C:\>_
```

1 Insert the **DESTINATION** floppy disk in drive **A:**

Note: Make sure the DESTI-NATION floppy disk does not contain any files.

2 Type **XCOPY C:\DATA A:/S** and press **Enter**.

■ The files and directories from hard drive **C:** are copied to the floppy disk in drive **A:**

■ When **C:\>** appears, **XCOPY** is complete.

COPY FILES AND DIRECTORIES FROM A FLOPPY DISK TO A HARD DISK

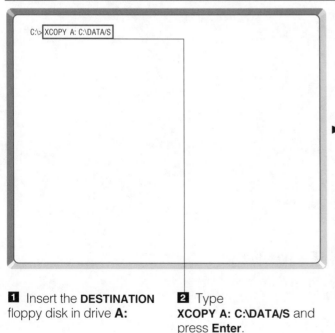

```
C:\> XCOPY A: C:\DATA/S
```

```
Reading source file(s)...
A:123DATA\INCOME1Q.WK1
A:123DATA\INCOME2Q.WK1
A:123DATA\INCOME3Q.WK1
A:123DATA\JIM.WK1
A:123DATA\PLAN1.WK1
A:123DATA\PLAN2.WK1
A:123DATA\PLAN3.WK1
A:123DATA\PROJECT1.WK1
A:123DATA\PROJECT2.WK1
A:123DATA\PROJECT3.WK1
A:WPDATA\1QPROFIT.MEM
A:WPDATA\2QPROFIT.MEM
A:WPDATA\3QPROFIT.MEM
A:WPDATA\DO_MON.LET
A:WPDATA\DO_TUES.LET
A:WPDATA\MERGE.LET
A:WPDATA\NOTE1Q.TXT
A:WPDATA\NOTE2Q.TXT
A:WPDATA\TEST.LET
A:WPDATA\TRAINING.LET
       20 File(s) copied
C:\>_
```

1 Insert the **DESTINATION** floppy disk in drive **A:**

2 Type **XCOPY A: C:\DATA/S** and press **Enter**.

■ The files and directories from floppy disk **A:** are copied to hard drive **C:**

■ When **C:\>** appears, **XCOPY** is complete.

CHECK DISK

The Check Disk command (typed as CHKDSK) is used to display the status of files and directories on a hard or floppy disk. It also displays the computer's electronic (or RAM) memory up to 640K and how much memory is available for running programs.

As a disk fills up, files are separated into units and given allocation identification numbers. A File Allocation Table keeps track of all the allocation units.

System or program problems can cause the table to lose track of some of these units, which are then called "open" files.

Check Disk identifies that "open" files exist. It does not try to recover them unless you have specified the /F switch.

Since CHKDSK is an external command, the Path command should include C:\DOS. During the installation of MS-DOS 5.0, the Path command C:\DOS is automatically installed in your AUTOEXEC.BAT file.

Note: If for some reason the Path command C:\DOS is not installed in your AUTOEXEC.BAT file, the current drive and directory must be changed to C:\DOS before issuing this command (refer to page 8).

The Check Disk command is:		
CHKDSK	DRIVE	/F
DRIVE		Tells MS-DOS the drive you want to check (A:, B:, or C:). If you do not specify a drive, MS-DOS checks the current drive.
/F		MS-DOS asks if you want to try to recover "open" files.

CHECK DISK AND MEMORY STATUS

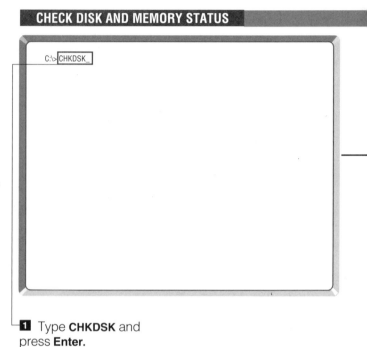

1 Type **CHKDSK** and press **Enter.**

FIX ERRORS ON THE DISK (/F)

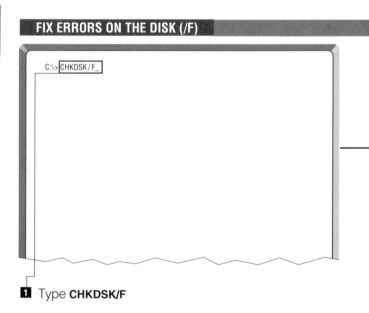

1 Type **CHKDSK/F**

Using the Command Prompt

Getting Started

Managing Your Directories

Managing Your Files

Managing Your Floppy Disks

Managing Your Hard Disk

```
C:\>CHKDSK

Volume  HARDDRIVE      created 03-22-1991 9:01p
Volume  Serial Number is 1679-791B
Error found, F parameter not specified
Corrections will not be written to the disk

        2 lost clusters found in 2 chains.
    4528    bytes disk space would be freed

33435648    bytes total disk space
    6144    bytes in 6 directories
14608464    bytes in 317 user files
18821040    bytes available on disk

    2048    bytes in each allocation unit
   16322    total allocation units on disk
    9226    available allocation units on disk

  655360    total bytes memory
  426368    bytes free

C:\>_
```

These lines tell you that there are errors in the File Allocation Table. To fix the errors, use the /F parameter described below. If no errors exist, these lines do not appear.

The amount of disk space occupied by "open" files.

The total amount of storage space on the disk.

The amount of memory occupied by the directories.

The number of programs and data files and the space they occupy.

The amount of disk space still available.

These lines tell you how much memory the computer has and how much of it is available for running programs.

■ MS-DOS displays the hard disk and computer memory status.

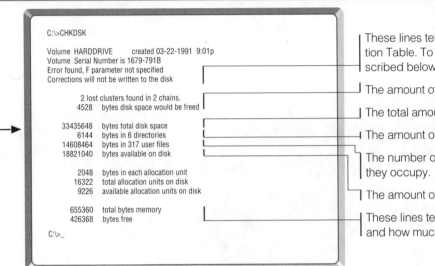

```
C:\>CHKDSK/F

Volume  HARDDRIVE      created 03-19-1991 4:43p
Volume  Serial Number is 1679-791B

 2 lost clusters found in 2 chains.
Convert lost chains to files (Y/N)? Y

33435648    bytes total disk space
   73728    bytes in 3 hidden files
    6144    bytes in 6 directories
14608464    bytes in 317 user files
18821040    bytes available on disk

    2048    bytes in each allocation unit
   16322    total allocation units on disk
    9226    available allocation units on disk

  655360    total bytes memory
  426368    bytes free
```

*Note: If you typed **Y** in Step 3, MS-DOS converts the "open" files into files named FILE0001.CHK, FILE0002.CHK, etc.*

These files are saved to the root directory. You can use the Type command to display their contents. If the files contain useful information, they should be kept.

However, if the information is of no value, delete the files to increase the storage capacity on your hard disk.

2 Press **Enter** and MS-DOS displays the message above if "open" files are detected.

3 Type **Y** and press **Enter** to fix the errors in the File Allocation Table.

or

Type **N** and press **Enter** to fix the disk, but not save the contents of the lost allocation units.

START THE
MS-DOS SHELL

1 To start the MS-DOS Shell, type **DOSSHELL** and press **Enter**.

C:\>DOSSHELL

CONVENTIONS

■ If key names are separated by a plus (+), press and hold down the first key before pressing the second key (example: **Shift+Tab**).

■ If key names are separated by a comma (,) press and release the first key before pressing the second key (example: **Alt,F**).

Note: To use a mouse with the MS-DOS Shell, install MOUSE.COM before starting the Shell. Refer to your Microsoft User's Guide.

Start the
MS-DOS Shell

Select
Commands

Change Screen
Mode

Change Color
Scheme

Help

THE MS-DOS SHELL

Most of the character based MS-DOS commands can be performed using the MS-DOS Shell.

The Shell provides a more efficient and practical method of organizing and starting application programs.

It also offers a new feature called "Task Swapper" which allows you to quickly switch between programs.

The **Disk Drive** area displays the computer's disk drives.

The **Directory Tree** area displays the directories on the current drive. The current directory is C:\

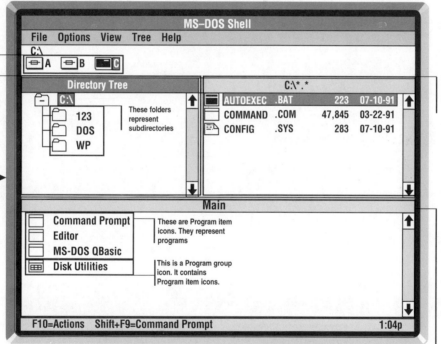

The **File** area lists all the files in the current directory.

The **Main** area lists all the programs installed on the computer.

Editor is used to create batch programs. MS-DOS QBasic is used to write Basic programs.

If this screen does not appear, press **Alt**,**V**,**F** to display it.

Note: If the graphics on the screen above do not match your display, refer to page 66 entitled "CHANGE SCREEN MODE and COLOR SCHEME".

TO SELECT AN AREA

To move from area to area, press **Tab**. The bar above the selected area is highlighted.

To move in the opposite direction, press **Shift**+**Tab**.

USING THE MOUSE

Move the mouse ⬚ anywhere in the area you want to select and click the left button.

Using the MS-DOS Shell

Getting Started

Managing Your Directories

Managing Your Programs

Managing Your Files

Disk Utilities

SELECT COMMANDS

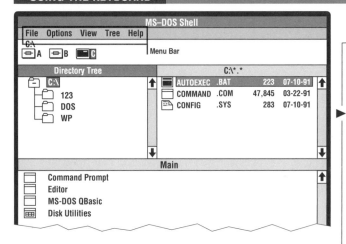

MS-DOS Shell commands are listed on the menus named File, Options, View, Tree and Help.

1 Press **F10** or **Alt** to highlight the **Menu Bar**.

■ The **File** menu is highlighted in the **Menu Bar**.

USING THE MOUSE

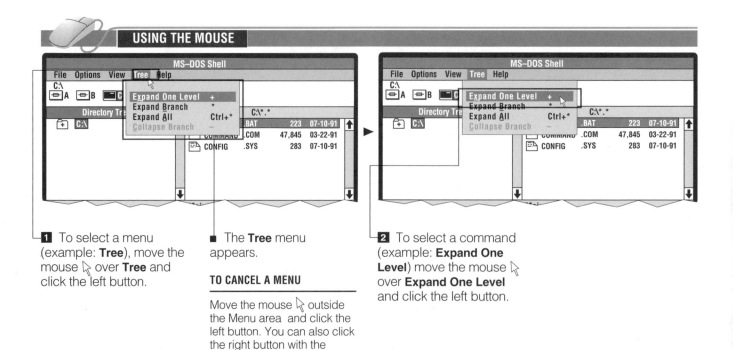

1 To select a menu (example: **Tree**), move the mouse ⌖ over **Tree** and click the left button.

■ The **Tree** menu appears.

TO CANCEL A MENU

Move the mouse ⌖ outside the Menu area and click the left button. You can also click the right button with the mouse ⌖ anywhere on the screen.

2 To select a command (example: **Expand One Level**) move the mouse ⌖ over **Expand One Level** and click the left button.

Start the
MS-DOS Shell

**Select
Commands**

Change Screen
Mode

Change Color
Scheme

Help

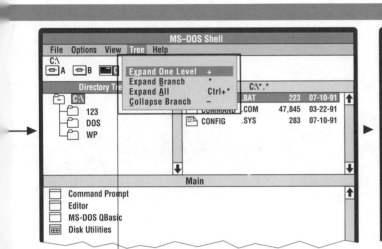

2 To select and open a
menu (example: **Tree**),
press ▶ 3 times.

*Note: To select any other
menu, press ▶ or ◀ until it
is highlighted.*

3 Then press **Enter** or ⬇.

TO CANCEL A MENU

Press **Esc**.

4 To select a command
(example: **Collapse
Branch**), press ⬇ 3 times.

*Note: To select any other
command, press ⬇ or ⬆
until it is highlighted.*

5 Then press **Enter**.

☞ **Shortcut**

To replace steps **1** to
5 , press **Alt,T,C**.

Using the
MS-DOS
Shell

**Getting
Started**

Managing
Your
Directories

Managing
Your
Programs

Managing
Your
Files

Disk
Utilities

USING KEYBOARD SHORTCUT

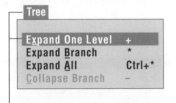

■ To select a menu
command (example:
Expand One Level), press
Alt,T,X.

T is the underlined letter
for the **T**ree menu and **x** is
the underlined letter for the
E**x**pand One Level
command.

*Note: MS-DOS commands are
not case sensitive. You can
press **Alt,T,X** or **Alt,t,x**.*

*Note: The dimmed command
is not currently operational. In
this example, Collapse Branch
is dimmed because the current
branch has already been
collapsed into the C:\ folder
(refer to "USING THE MOUSE"
on page 64).*

DESCRIPTIVE SHORTCUTS

For the rest of this
guide, the following
shortcuts are used:

■ "Move the mouse ▷
over **xx** and click the
left button" becomes:

Click xx.

■ "Move the mouse ▷
over **xx** and click the
left button twice in
quick succession"
becomes:

Double click xx.

CHANGE SCREEN MODE FROM TEXT TO GRAPHICS

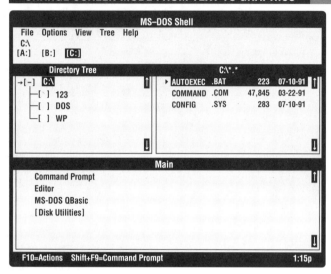

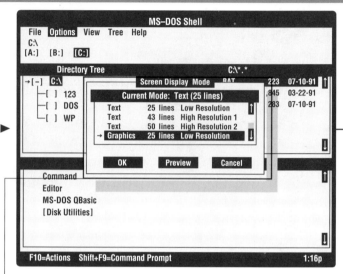

When you first start the MS-DOS Shell, the screen display above appears.

If your computer has color graphics capability, we recommend that you change:

– screen mode from text to graphics 25 lines low resolution

and

– color scheme from monochrome-2 colors to monochrome-4 colors or any color displayed on the Color Scheme dialog box.

1 Press **Alt,O,D** and the **Screen Display Mode** dialog box appears.

2 Press ⬇ 3 times to select **Graphics 25 lines Low Resolution**.

*Note: To preview your selection, Press **Tab** until the cursor is in the **Preview** button. Then press **Enter**.*

3 To save the new Screen Display Mode, press **Enter**.

USING THE MOUSE

1. Click **Options** to open its menu.

2. Click **Display** and the **Screen Display Mode** dialog box appears.

3. Click **Graphics 25 lines Low Resolution**.

*Note: To preview your selection, click the **Preview** button.*

4. To save the new Screen Display Mode, click the **OK** button.

Start the
MS-DOS Shell

Select
Commands

Change
Screen Mode

Change Color
Scheme

Help

CHANGE COLOR SCHEME

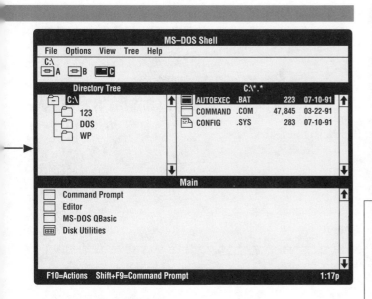

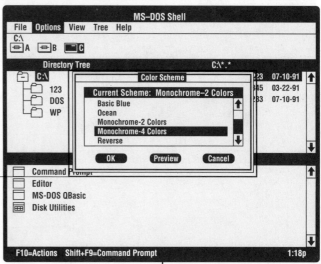

■ The **Graphics 25 lines Low Resolution** Screen Display Mode is displayed.

1 Press **Alt,O,O** and the **Color Scheme** dialog box appears.

2 Press [↓] to select **Monochrome-4 Colors**.

*Note: To preview your selection, press **Tab** until the cursor is in the **Preview** button. Then press **Enter**.*

3 To save the new Color Scheme, press **Enter**.

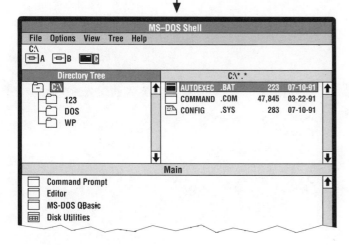

USING THE MOUSE

1. Click **Options** to open its menu.

2. Click **Colors** and the **Color Scheme** dialog box appears.

3. Click **Monochrome-4 Colors**.

*Note: To preview your selection, click the **Preview** button.*

4. To save the **Mono-chrome-4 Colors** Color Scheme, click the **OK** button.

■ The **Monochrome-4 Colors** Color Scheme is displayed.

Using the MS-DOS Shell

Getting Started

Managing Your Directories

Managing Your Programs

Managing Your Files

Disk Utilities

GETTING HELP ON COMMANDS AND PROCEDURES

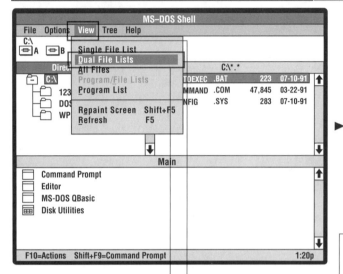

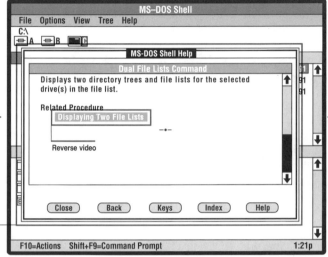

On-line Help is available for all commands and procedures listed in the menus.

1 Select a menu (example: Press **Alt,V** to select the **View** menu).

2 Highlight a command (example: press ⬇ to highlight **Dual File Lists**).

3 Press **F1** to get help on the highlighted command.

4 Press **Enter** to get help on **Displaying Two File Lists**.

*Note: In some Help screens more than one item is displayed in reverse video. Press **Tab** until the item you require is selected. Then press **Enter**.*

TO CANCEL HELP AT ANY TIME

Press **Esc**.

USING THE MOUSE

1. Click **View** to open its menu.

2. Press ⬇ to highlight **Dual File Lists**.

3. Press **F1**.

4. Double click **Displaying Two File Lists**.

• If more than one item is displayed in reverse video, double click the one you want to get help on.

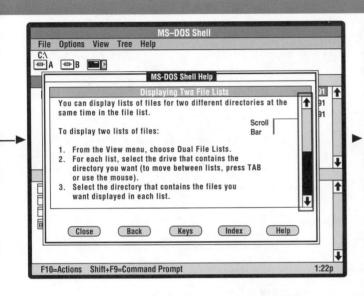

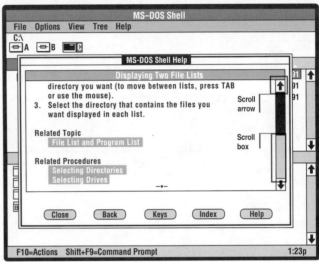

■ Proceed to step **5**.

or

Press **Tab** until the cursor is in the button function you want. Then press **Enter**.

BUTTON FUNCTIONS

Close   Returns you to the MS-DOS Shell.

Back   Moves you back one screen.

Keys   Gives you help on keyboard operations.

Index   Gives you help on using the MS-DOS Shell.

Help   Gives you help on using Help.

5 Press **Page Down** to display the above screen.

USING THE SCROLL BAR

If a Scroll bar contains a Scroll box, more information is available. If the Scroll box is small, you are currently viewing only a small part of the information available. If the Scroll box is large, you are currently viewing most of the information available.

Press ⬇ or ⬆	Scrolls the screen one line down or up.
Press Page Down or Page Up	Scrolls down or up one whole screen.
Press Home	Scrolls to the top of the information.
Press End	Scrolls to the end of the information.

• Proceed to step **5**.

or

Click the button function you want.

5. Move the mouse ⬏ over the scroll box. Click the left button and hold it down. Still holding down the button, drag the Scroll box to the end of the Scroll bar. Release the button.

Note: For screens with more information, drag the Scroll box until the information required appears.

Click the top or bottom scroll arrows	Scrolls the screen one line up or down.

Using the
MS-DOS
Shell

Getting
Started

Managing
Your
Directories

Managing
Your
Programs

Managing
Your
Files

Disk
Utilities

CHANGE DISK DRIVES

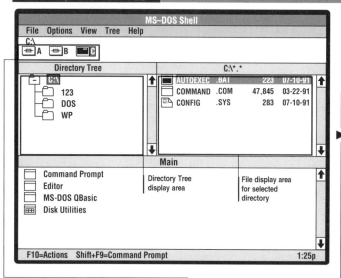

The **Directory Tree** area of the screen displays the directories on the current drive.

Folders are graphic representations of directories.

1 Press **Tab** until the **Disk Drive** area is selected.

2 To change to another drive (example: drive **A:**), press ← twice and press **Enter**.

☞ Shortcut

To change to drive **A:**, press **Ctrl+A**.

To change to drive **B:**, press **Ctrl+B**.

■ The **Directory Tree** displays the directory structure of the floppy disk in drive **A:**

3 To change the current drive back to drive **C:**, press **Ctrl+C**.

Note: In this example, the floppy disk in drive A: does not contain files or subdirectories.

USING THE MOUSE

1. Click the disk drive icon **A** or **B** (example: ⊟A or ⊟B).

2. Click disk drive icon **C** to change the current drive back to drive **C:**

Change
Disk Drives

Change
Directories

Create
Directories

Expand or Collapse
Directory Levels

Delete
Directories

Show
Information

CHANGE DIRECTORIES

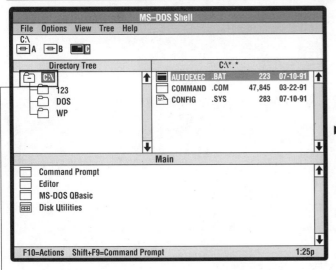

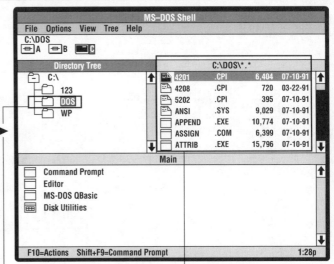

■ The current directory is identified by the high-lighted folder name (**C:**).

1 Press **Tab** until the **Directory Tree** area is selected.

2 To change to another directory (example: **DOS**) press ⬇ until the **DOS** folder is selected.

■ The current directory is now **\\DOS** and its files are displayed in the **File** area.

USING THE MOUSE

1. Click the folder (example: **DOS**) of the directory you want to change to.

KEYBOARD SHORTCUTS

Press	Resulting action
↑ or ↓	Move up or down one directory
Home	Move to the root directory
End	Move to the last directory
Page Up	Move one directory window up from the current directory
Page Dn	Move one directory window down from the current directory
Type the first letter of the directory name	Move to the directory starting with that letter

USING THE NUMERIC KEYPAD

To use the numeric keypad's arrows, PgUp, PgDn, Home and End keys, **Num Lock** must be **off**.

If the **NumLock** status light is **on**, press **Num Lock** to turn it **off**.

Using the
MS-DOS
Shell

Getting
Started

Managing
Your
Directories

Managing
Your
Programs

Managing
Your
Files

Disk
Utilities

CREATE DIRECTORIES

All examples in this guide are based on the directory structure illustrated below:

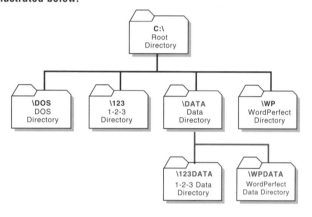

CREATE THE \DATA DIRECTORY

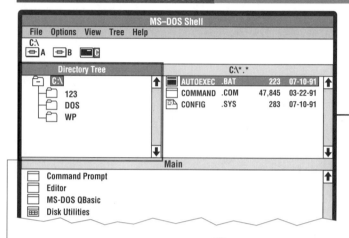

1 Press **Tab** until the **Directory Tree** area is selected.

2 Press ⬆ until the **root directory (C:\)** is selected.

3 Press **Alt,F,E**, to access the **Create Directory** dialog box.

USING THE MOUSE

1. Click the **root directory (C:\)** to select it.

2. Click **File** to open its menu.

3. Click **Create Directory**.

CREATE THE 123DATA AND WPDATA DIRECTORIES

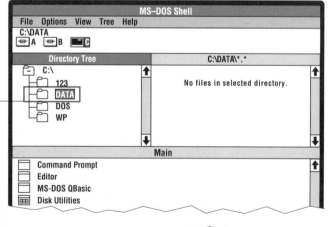

1 Press **Tab** until the **Directory Tree** area is selected.

2 Press ⬇ or ⬆ to select the **DATA** folder.

3 Press **Alt,F,E**, to access the **Create Directory** dialog box.

USING THE MOUSE

1. Click the **DATA** folder to select it.

2. Click **File** to open its menu.

3. Click **Create Directory**.

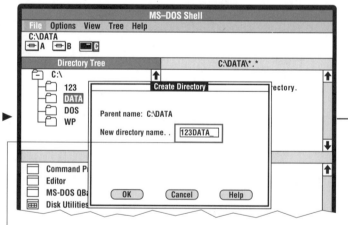

4 Type the name of the new directory (example: **123DATA**) and press **Enter**.

USING THE MOUSE

4. Type **123DATA** and click the **OK** button.

Change
Disk Drives

Change
Directories

Create
Directories

Expand or Collapse
Directory Levels

Delete
Directories

Show
Information

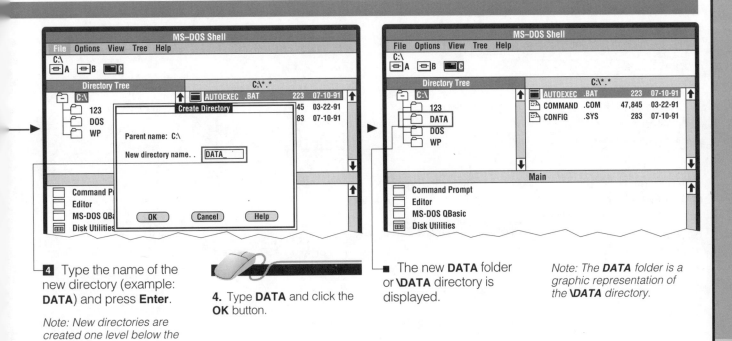

4 Type the name of the new directory (example: **DATA**) and press **Enter**.

Note: New directories are created one level below the current directory. In this example, the current directory is C:

4. Type **DATA** and click the **OK** button.

■ The new **DATA** folder or **\DATA** directory is displayed.

*Note: The **DATA** folder is a graphic representation of the **\DATA** directory.*

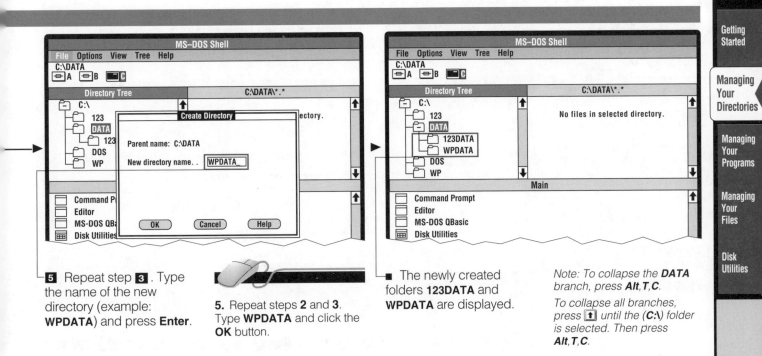

5 Repeat step **3**. Type the name of the new directory (example: **WPDATA**) and press **Enter**.

5. Repeat steps **2** and **3**. Type **WPDATA** and click the **OK** button.

■ The newly created folders **123DATA** and **WPDATA** are displayed.

*Note: To collapse the **DATA** branch, press **Alt,T,C**.*

*To collapse all branches, press ⬆ until the (**C:**) folder is selected. Then press **Alt,T,C**.*

Using the
MS–DOS
Shell

Getting
Started

Managing
Your
Directories

Managing
Your
Programs

Managing
Your
Files

Disk
Utilities

EXPAND OR COLLAPSE
DIRECTORY LEVELS

EXPAND ONE LEVEL OF A DIRECTORY

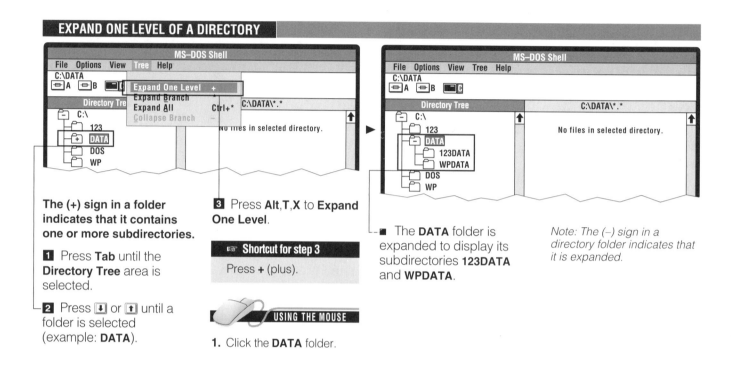

The (+) sign in a folder indicates that it contains one or more subdirectories.

1 Press **Tab** until the **Directory Tree** area is selected.

2 Press ⬇ or ⬆ until a folder is selected (example: **DATA**).

3 Press **Alt,T,X** to **Expand One Level**.

☞ **Shortcut for step 3**

Press **+** (plus).

USING THE MOUSE

1. Click the **DATA** folder.

■ The **DATA** folder is expanded to display its subdirectories **123DATA** and **WPDATA**.

Note: The (–) sign in a directory folder indicates that it is expanded.

EXPAND AN ENTIRE DIRECTORY BRANCH

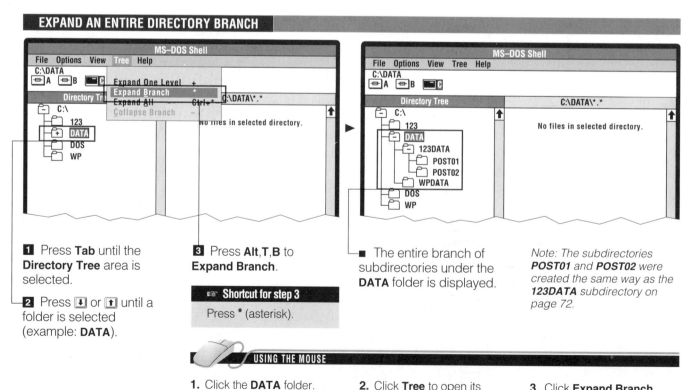

1 Press **Tab** until the **Directory Tree** area is selected.

2 Press ⬇ or ⬆ until a folder is selected (example: **DATA**).

3 Press **Alt,T,B** to **Expand Branch**.

☞ **Shortcut for step 3**

Press ***** (asterisk).

USING THE MOUSE

1. Click the **DATA** folder.

■ The entire branch of subdirectories under the **DATA** folder is displayed.

Note: The subdirectories POST01 and POST02 were created the same way as the 123DATA subdirectory on page 72.

2. Click **Tree** to open its menu.

3. Click **Expand Branch**.

Change
Disk Drives

Change
Directories

Create
Directories

**Expand or Collapse
Directory Levels**

Delete
Directories

Show
Information

EXPAND ALL BRANCHES

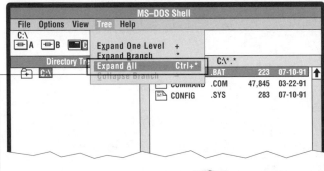

```
                    MS–DOS Shell
 File  Options  View  Tree  Help
 C:\
 [=]A  [=]B  [=]C
                    Expand One Level   +
        Directory Tre Expand Branch    *      C:\*.*
 [📁] C:\          Expand All   Ctrl+*    .BAT    223   07-10-91  ↑
                    Collapse Branch          COMMAND   .COM   47,845  03-22-91
                                             CONFIG    .SYS      283  07-10-91
```

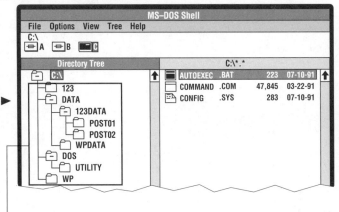

```
                    MS–DOS Shell
 File  Options  View  Tree  Help
 C:\
 [=]A  [=]B  [=]C
        Directory Tree                       C:\*.*
 [📁] C:\                            ↑   AUTOEXEC  .BAT    223   07-10-91  ↑
         [📁] 123                            COMMAND   .COM   47,845  03-22-91
         [📁] DATA                           CONFIG    .SYS      283  07-10-91
              [📁] 123DATA
                   [📁] POST01
                   [📁] POST02
              [📁] WPDATA
         [📁] DOS
              [📁] UTILITY
         [📁] WP
```

1 Press **Tab** until the **Directory Tree** area is selected.

2 Press **Alt,T,A** to **Expand All** branches.

▸ Click **Tree** to open its menu.

2. Click **Expand All**.

☞ **Shortcut for step 2**

Press **Ctrl**+*.

■ All subdirectories are displayed.

*Note: The subdirectory **UTILITY** was created the same way as the **123DATA** subdirectory on page 72.*

COLLAPSE A BRANCH

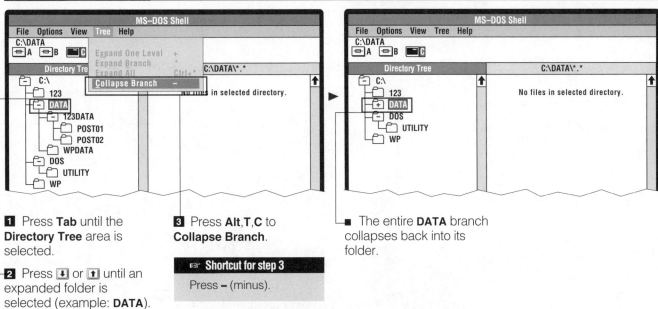

```
                    MS–DOS Shell
 File  Options  View  Tree  Help
 C:\DATA
 [=]A  [=]B  [=]C
        Directory Tre Expand One Level   +
 [📁] C:\          Expand Branch    *   C:\DATA\*.*
         [📁] 123    Expand All   Ctrl+*
         [📁] DATA   Collapse Branch  –   No files in selected directory.
              [📁] 123DATA
                   [📁] POST01
                   [📁] POST02
              [📁] WPDATA
         [📁] DOS
              [📁] UTILITY
         [📁] WP
```

```
                    MS–DOS Shell
 File  Options  View  Tree  Help
 C:\DATA
 [=]A  [=]B  [=]C
        Directory Tree                  C:\DATA\*.*
 [📁] C:\                         ↑   No files in selected directory.
         [📁] 123
         [+] DATA
         [📁] DOS
              [📁] UTILITY
         [📁] WP
```

1 Press **Tab** until the **Directory Tree** area is selected.

2 Press [↓] or [↑] until an expanded folder is selected (example: **DATA**).

3 Press **Alt,T,C** to **Collapse Branch**.

☞ **Shortcut for step 3**

Press **–** (minus).

▸ USING THE MOUSE

1. Click the **DATA** folder to collapse its branch.

*Note: To collapse all branches, click the **C:** folder.*

■ The entire **DATA** branch collapses back into its folder.

Using the
MS-DOS
Shell

Getting
Started

Managing
Your
Directories

Managing
Your
Programs

Managing
Your
Files

Disk
Utilities

DELETE DIRECTORIES

DELETE A DIRECTORY

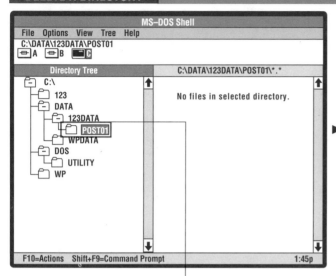

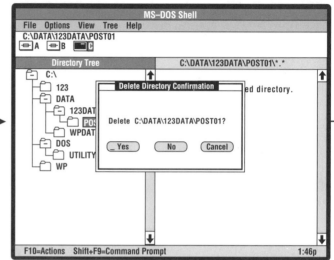

1 Press **Alt,V,S** to display the **Single File List** view.

2 Press **Tab** until the **Directory Tree** area is selected.

3 Press **Ctrl+*** to expand all branches.

4 Press ⬇ or ⬆ until an expanded folder is selected (example: **POST01**).

5 Press **Alt,F,D** to delete the selected directory

☞ **Shortcut for step 5**

Press **Delete**.

■ The **Delete Directory Confirmation** dialog box appears.

6 To delete the selected directory, press **Enter**.

or

To cancel the command, press **Tab** until the cursor is in the **Cancel** button. Then press **Enter**.

USING THE MOUSE

1. Click **View** to open its menu.

2. Click **Single File List** to view it.

3. Click the **DATA** folder to open it.

4. Click the **123DATA** folder to open it.

5. Click the **POST01** folder to select it.

6. Click **File** to open its menu.

7. Click **Delete**.

• The **Delete Directory Confirmation** dialog box appears.

8. To delete the selected directory, click the **Yes** button.

or

To cancel the command, click the **Cancel** button.

CHECK OR CHANGE FILE OPTIONS

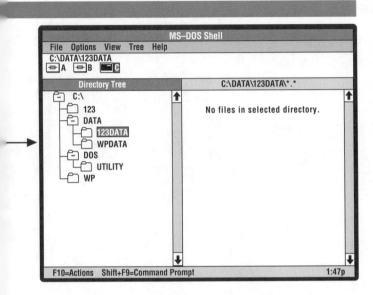

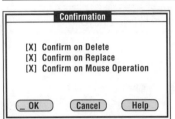

■ The **POST01** folder or directory is deleted.

Note: If a directory contains files or subdirectories, a **Deletion Error** *dialog box appears.*

This warning dialog box alerts you that the directory you are trying to delete contains files or subdirectories.

All files and subdirectories in the selected directory must be deleted before the directory can be deleted.

Refer to page 114 to learn how to delete files.

1 To access the **Confirmation** dialog box, press **Alt,O,C**.

2 To move through the options in its dialog box, press **Tab**.

3 To toggle between **on [X]** and **off [ ]**, press **Spacebar**.

4 To save changes, press **Enter**. To get help, press **Tab** until the cursor is in the **Help** button. Then press **Enter**.

USING THE MOUSE

1. Click **Options** to open its menu.

2. Click **Confirmation** to access its dialog box.

3. To toggle a File Option between **on [X]** and **off [ ]**, click its box.

4. To save changes, click the **OK** button. To cancel changes, click the **Cancel** button. To get help, click the **Help** button.

Note: We recommend you keep all Confirmation options **on**. *Then each time you delete files or directories, or use the mouse to copy or move files—the* **Confirmation** *dialog box appears. This allows you one last chance to change your mind before deleting files or subdirectories.*

Using the
MS-DOS
Shell

Getting
Started

Managing
Your
Directories

Managing
Your
Programs

Managing
Your
Files

Disk
Utilities

SHOW
INFORMATION

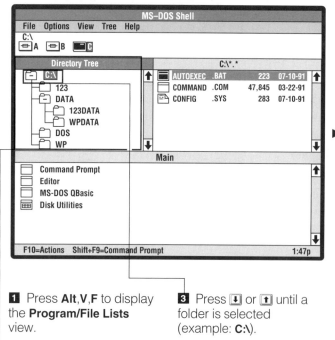

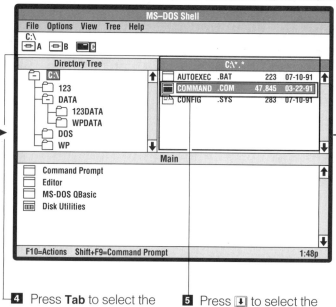

1 Press **Alt,V,F** to display the **Program/File Lists** view.

2 Press **Tab** to select the **Directory Tree** area.

3 Press ↓ or ↑ until a folder is selected (example: **C:**).

4 Press **Tab** to select the **File** area.

5 Press ↓ to select the **COMMAND.COM** file.

SELECT A FILE

Press ↓	To select a file below the current file.
Press ↑	To select a file above the current file.
Press End	To select the last file.
Press Home	To select the first file.
Press the first letter of the filename	To select the first file starting with that letter.

 USING THE MOUSE

1. Click **View** to open its menu.

2. Click **Program/File Lists** to display its screen.

3. Click the **C:** folder to select it.

4. Click the file you want information on (example: **COMMAND.COM**).

Change
Disk Drives

Change
Directories

Create
Directories

Expand or Collapse
Directory Levels

Delete
Directories

**Show
Information**

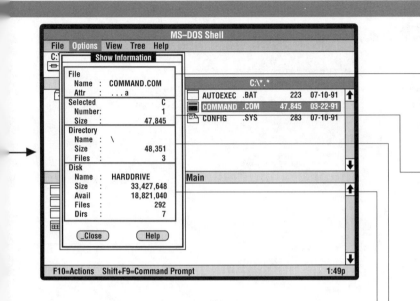

File

Information on the selected file
(**COMMAND.COM**) is displayed. A file
attribute defines the kind of file it is. The file
attribute can be (a) archive, (r) read-only,
(h) hidden, or (s) system.

*Note: Refer to the Microsoft User's Guide
for an explanation of file attributes (for
advanced users).*

Selected

Displays the number of selected files (**1**)
and size in bytes (**47,845**). More than one
file can be selected (refer to page 92). The
size is the sum of all the selected files.

*Note: If you switch between two disks, two
columns appear in the selected area. One
column is the recently selected disk and the
other is the previously selected disk. The
size displays the sum of all selected files on
both disks.*

Directory

Displays the name (\ or root directory), size
in bytes (**48,351**), and number of files in the
directory (**3**).

Disk

Displays information on the disk containing
the selected file, including name
(**HARDDRIVE**), size in bytes (**33,427,648**),
number of files and directories (**292** and **7**)
and disk space available in bytes
(**18,821,040**).

6 Press **Alt,O,S** to select
the **Show Information**
dialog box.

*Note: The dialog box displays
full details of the selected file,
its directory and disk drive.*

7 Press **Enter** to close
the dialog box.

5. Click **Options** to open its
menu.

6. Click **Show Information**
to display its dialog box.

7. Click the **Close** button to
close the dialog box.

Using the
MS-DOS
Shell

Getting
Started

Managing
Your
Directories

Managing
Your
Programs

Managing
Your
Files

Disk
Utilities

START A PROGRAM

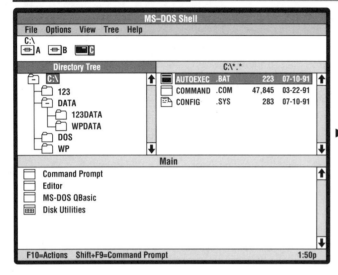

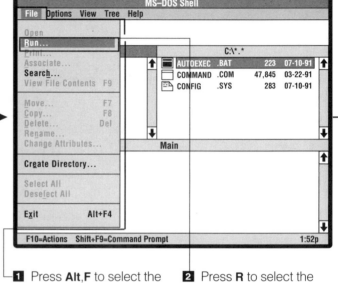

The Run command allows you to start application programs (example: Lotus 1-2-3, and WordPerfect) directly from the MS-DOS Shell.

Note: In the examples that follow, we are assuming that:

Lotus 1-2-3 resides in a directory named C:\123.

and

WordPerfect resides in a directory named C:\WP.

1 Press **Alt,F** to select the **File** menu.

2 Press **R** to select the **Run** command. Its dialog box appears on the next screen.

USING THE MOUSE

1. Click **File** to open its menu.

2. Click **Run** and its dialog box appears on the next screen.

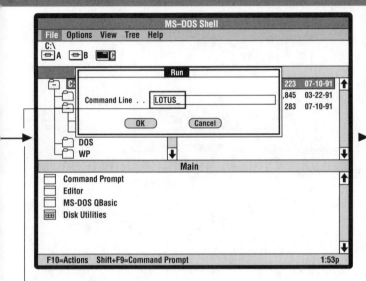

```
                    MS–DOS Shell
  File  Options  View  Tree  Help
  C:\
  ⬚A   ⬚B   ⬛C
  ┌─────────────────Run──────────────────┐    223  07-10-91  ↑
  🗁 C:│                                  │   ,845  03-22-91
    🗁 │  Command Line . .  │LOTUS_     │     283  07-10-91
    🗁 │                                  │
       │        ( OK )        ( Cancel )   │
    🗁 DOS                                          ↓
    🗁 WP                                           ↓
  ──────────────────Main──────────────────
  🗋  Command Prompt                               ↑
  🗋  Editor
  🗋  MS-DOS QBasic
  🖩  Disk Utilities

                                                  ↓
  F10=Actions   Shift+F9=Command Prompt            1:53p
```

3 Type **LOTUS** (the
program startup command
for Lotus 1-2-3) and press
Enter.

*Note: The startup command
for the WordPerfect program
is **WP**.*

*Note: Check your path
command (refer to page 11).
If it does not include the drive
and path to the program, they
must be included in the Run
Command line.*

*For example, to start Lotus
1-2-3 without a drive and path
specified in the path command, type **C:\123\LOTUS**
and press **Enter**.*

3. Type **LOTUS** and click
the **OK** button.

```
┌──────────────────────────────────────────┐
│ 1-2-3   PrintGraph   Translate   Install   Exit │
│ Use 1-2-3                                        │
├──────────────────────────────────────────┤
│                                            │
│           1-2-3 Access System              │
│         Copyright  1986, 1989              │
│       Lotus Development Corporation        │
│            All Rights Reserved             │
│              Release 2.2                    │
│                                            │
│  The Access system lets you choose 1-2-3, PrintGraph, the Translate utility, │
│  and the Install program, from the menu at the top of this screen.  If │
│  you're using a two-diskette system, the Access system may prompt you to │
│  change disks.  Follow the instructions below to start a program. │
│                                            │
│  ○  Use → or ← to move the menu pointer (the highlighted rectangle │
│      at the top of the screen) to the program you want to use. │
│                                            │
│  ○  Press ENTER to start the program.      │
│                                            │
│  You can also start a program by typing the first character of its name. │
│                                            │
│  Press HELP (F1) for more information.     │
│                                            │
└──────────────────────────────────────────┘
```

■ The Lotus **1-2-3 Access
System** screen appears.

*Note: If you are using
another program, check its
User Manual for its startup
command. The extension
(.EXE) does not have to be
included in the Run
Command Line.*

Using the
MS-DOS
Shell

Getting
Started

Managing
Your
Directories

Managing
Your
Programs

Managing
Your
Files

Disk
Utilities

ADD A PROGRAM ITEM ICON TO THE MAIN AREA

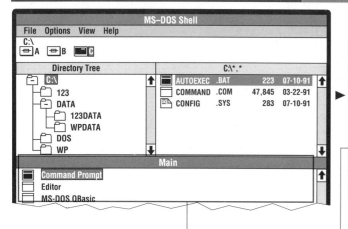

To start a program (example: WordPerfect) from the MS-DOS Shell, its Program item icon must be added to the Main area.

1 Press **Tab** until the **Main** area is selected.

2 Press **Alt,F,N** to access the **New Program Object** dialog box.

1. Click in the **Main** area to select it.

2. Click **File** to open its menu.

3. Click **New** to access the **New Program Object** dialog box.

START A PROGRAM FROM ITS PROGRAM ITEM ICON

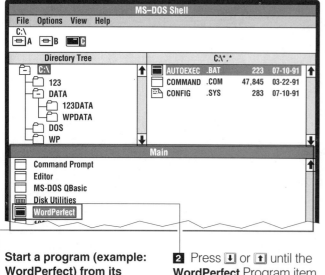

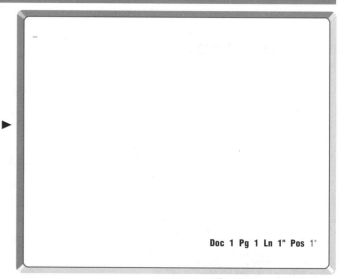

Doc 1 Pg 1 Ln 1" Pos 1"

Start a program (example: WordPerfect) from its Program item icon in the Main area.

1 Press **Tab** until the **Main** area is selected.

2 Press ⬇ or ⬆ until the **WordPerfect** Program item icon is selected.

3 Press **Enter**. **WordPerfect** starts and displays its opening screen.

1. Double click the **WordPerfect** program item.

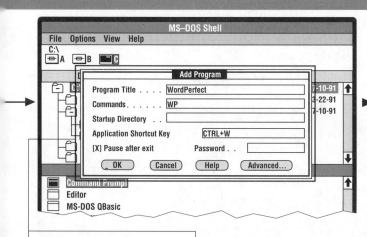

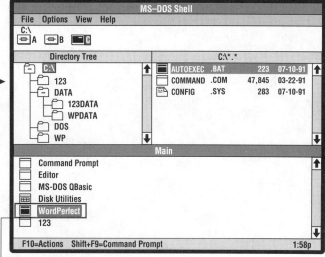

3 Press **Enter** and the **Add Program** dialog box appears.

4 In the **Program Title** box, type the name (example: **WordPerfect**) that you want to appear in the **Main** area.

■ The **WordPerfect Program item icon** is displayed in the **Main** area.

Note: To add a Program item icon for Lotus 1-2-3, repeat steps **1** to **7** except:

– type **123** in step **4**

– type **LOTUS** in step **5**

– type **Ctrl+1** in step **6**

4. Click the **OK** button and the **Add Program** dialog box appears.

5. Type **WordPerfect**.

6. Click in the **Commands** box and then Type **WP**.

7. Click in the **Application Shortcut Key** box. Hold down **Ctrl** while you press **W**.

8. Click the **OK** button.

Note: Refer to the notes under steps **5** and **6**.

To add a Program item icon for Lotus 1-2-3, repeat steps **1.** to **8.** except:

- type **123** in step **5.**

- type **LOTUS** in step **6.**

- type **Ctrl+1** in step **7.**

5 Press **Tab** or ⬇ to move the cursor to the **Commands** box. Type **WP** (the startup command for WordPerfect).

Note: If the startup command is not in the current directory or the path command does not include C:\WP, type C:\WP\WP in the Commands box.

6 Press ⬇ twice to move to the **Application Shortcut Key** box. To create a shortcut key, hold down **Ctrl** while you press **W**. This simplifies starting the program as you will see on page 86.

Note: Shortcut keys are created by pressing Ctrl+character, Shift+character, or Alt+character. A character can be any letter, number or function key. Some key combinations are reserved by the system.

7 Press **Enter**.

Using the MS-DOS Shell

Getting Started

Managing Your Directories

Managing Your Programs

Managing Your Files

Disk Utilities

SWITCH BETWEEN PROGRAMS

ENABLE THE TASK SWAPPER

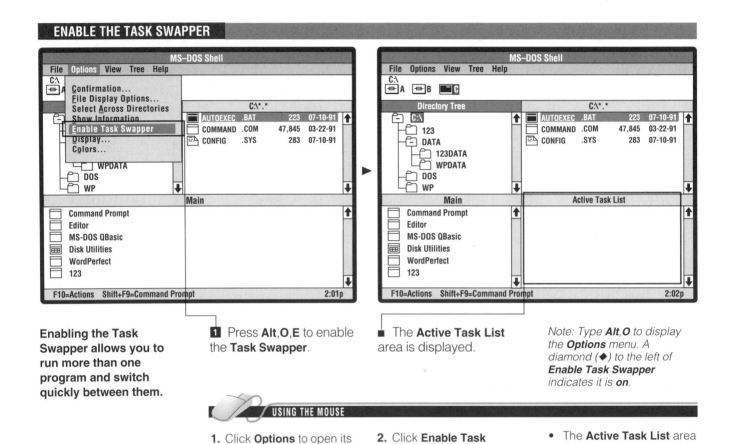

Enabling the Task Swapper allows you to run more than one program and switch quickly between them.

1 Press **Alt,O,E** to enable the **Task Swapper**.

■ The **Active Task List** area is displayed.

*Note: Type **Alt,O** to display the **Options** menu. A diamond (♦) to the left of **Enable Task Swapper** indicates it is **on**.*

USING THE MOUSE

1. Click **Options** to open its menu.

2. Click **Enable Task Swapper**.

• The **Active Task List** area is displayed.

USING THE PROGRAM LIST VIEW

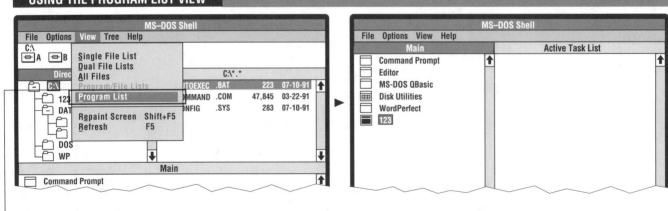

1 To switch to the **Program List** view, press **Alt,V,P**.

■ The **Program List** view is used when you work with a lot of Program item icons.

Start a
Program

**Switch Between
Programs**

Quit the
MS-DOS Shell

ADD PROGRAM ITEMS TO THE ACTIVE TASK LIST

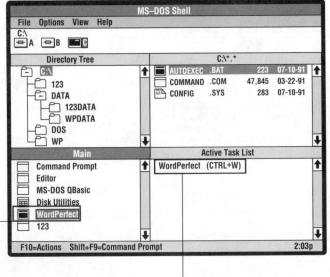

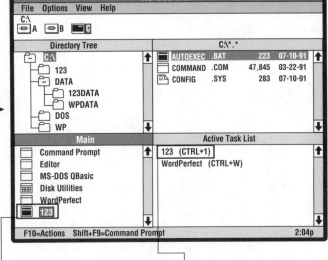

1 Press **Tab** until the **Main** area is selected.

2 Press ⬇ or ⬆ to select a Program item icon (example: **WordPerfect**) you want to add to the **Active Task List**.

3 Press **Shift+Enter** to add **WordPerfect** to the **Active Task List**.

4 Press ⬇ or ⬆ to select another Program item icon (example: **123**) that you want to add to the **Active Task List**.

5 Press **Shift+Enter** to add **123** to the **Active Task List**.

USING THE MOUSE

1. Click the Program item icon (example: **WordPerfect**) that you want to add to the **Active Task List**.

2. Press **Shift+Enter** to add **WordPerfect** to the **Active Task List**.

☞ **Shortcut**

To replace steps **1** and **2**, hold **Shift** down while you double click **WordPerfect**.

3. Click the Program item icon (example: **123**) that you want to add to the **Active Task List**.

4. Press **Shift+Enter** to add **123** to the **Active Task List**.

☞ **Shortcut**

To replace steps **3** and **4**, hold **Shift** down while you double click **123**.

Using the
MS-DOS
Shell

Getting
Started

Managing
Your
Directories

**Managing
Your
Programs**

Managing
Your
Files

Disk
Utilities

SWITCH BETWEEN PROGRAMS

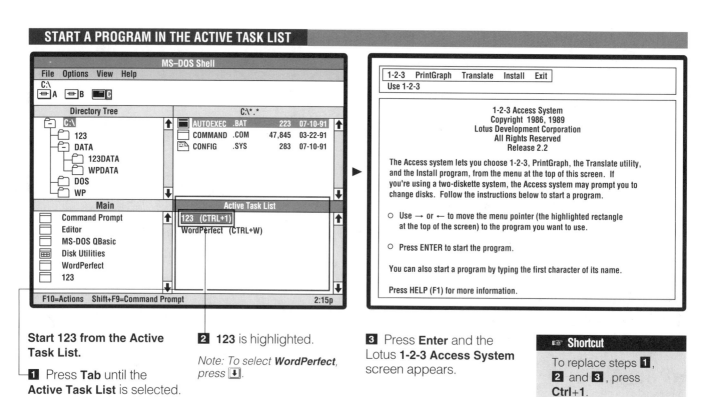

Start 123 from the Active Task List.

1 Press **Tab** until the **Active Task List** is selected.

2 **123** is highlighted.

*Note: To select **WordPerfect**, press ⬇.*

3 Press **Enter** and the Lotus **1-2-3 Access System** screen appears.

☞ **Shortcut**

To replace steps **1**, **2** and **3**, press **Ctrl+1**.

USING THE MOUSE

1. Double click the program you want to run or start (example: **123**).

• The Lotus **1-2-3 Access System** screen appears.

UPDATE THE SCREEN

If you add or delete files/directories in a program running in the MS-DOS Shell, these changes are not reflected when you return to the MS-DOS Shell.

To update the screen, press **F5** when the Menu Bar, Directory Tree or File area is selected.

*Note: "UPDATE THE SCREEN" will **not** work with the Main or Active Task List Area selected.*

REPAINT THE SCREEN

A terminate-and-stay resident (TSR) program running in the MS-DOS Shell may still appear on the screen after you quit the TSR program.

To return to the MS-DOS Shell screen, press **Shift+F5**.

Start a
Program

**Switch Between
Programs**

Quit the
MS-DOS Shell

SWITCH BETWEEN PROGRAMS IN THE ACTIVE TASK LIST

```
1-2-3   PrintGraph   Translate   Install   Exit
Use 1-2-3
```

1-2-3 Access System
Copyright 1986, 1989
Lotus Development Corporation
All Rights Reserved
Release 2.2

The Access system lets you choose 1-2-3, PrintGraph, the Translate utility,
and the Install program, from the menu at the top of this screen. If
you're using a two-diskette system, the Access system may prompt you to
change disks. Follow the instructions below to start a program.

○ Use → or ← to move the menu pointer (the highlighted rectangle
   at the top of the screen) to the program you want to use.

○ Press ENTER to start the program.

You can also start a program by typing the first character of its name.

Press HELP (F1) for more information.

1 To switch between
programs, hold down **Alt**
while you press **Tab**.

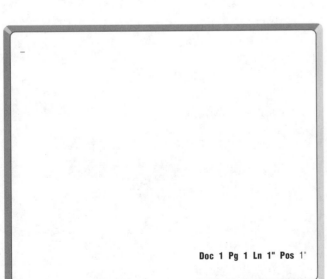

■ The **WordPerfect**
starting screen appears.

Doc 1 Pg 1 Ln 1" Pos 1"

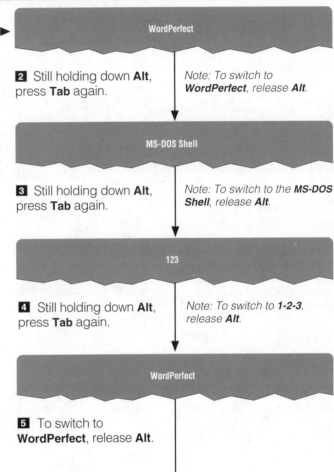

2 Still holding down **Alt**,
press **Tab** again.

*Note: To switch to
WordPerfect, release Alt.*

3 Still holding down **Alt**,
press **Tab** again.

*Note: To switch to the MS-DOS
Shell, release Alt.*

4 Still holding down **Alt**,
press **Tab** again.

*Note: To switch to 1-2-3,
release Alt.*

5 To switch to
WordPerfect, release **Alt**.

*Note: If you want to switch
back to 123, hold down Alt
and press Tab until 123
appears on the top of the
screen. Then release Alt.*

*To switch back to the
MS-DOS Shell from any
program, press Ctrl+Esc.*

Using the
MS-DOS
Shell

Getting
Started

Managing
Your
Directories

**Managing
Your
Programs**

Managing
Your
Files

Disk
Utilities

◀ 87

QUIT THE MS-DOS SHELL

LEAVE THE MS-DOS SHELL TEMPORARILY

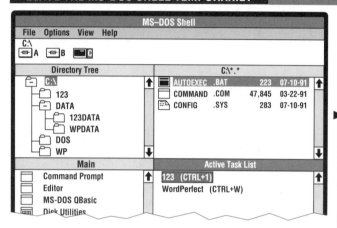

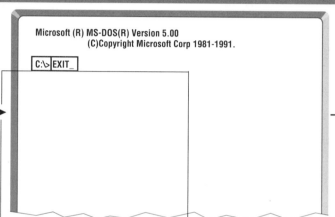

You can return to the command prompt (C:\>) and execute MS-DOS commands with Task Switching enabled.

1 Press **Shift+F9**.

USING THE MOUSE

1. Double click **Command Prompt** in the **Main** area.

■ The command prompt C:\> appears. MS-DOS commands can now be executed.

2 To return to the MS-DOS Shell, type **Exit** and press **Enter**.

☞ **Shortcut for step 2**

Hold down **Alt** and press **Esc**.

QUIT THE MS-DOS SHELL

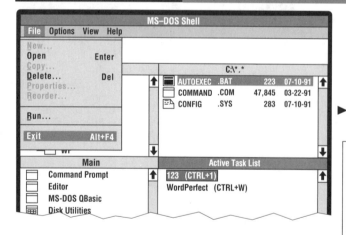

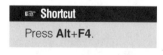

To quit the MS-DOS Shell completely and return to the command prompt C:\>, you must first quit all programs in the Active Task List.

1 Press **Alt,F,X**.

☞ **Shortcut**

Press **Alt+F4**.

USING THE MOUSE

1. Click **File** to open its menu.

2. Click **Exit**.

■ If programs are listed in the **Active Task List**, the **Exiting Error** dialog box appears.

• If programs are listed in the **Active Task List**, the **Exiting Error** dialog box appears.

2 Press **Enter** and then quit all programs in the **Active Task List** using their exit commands.

3. Click the **Close** button and then quit all programs in the **Active Task List** using their exit commands.

88 ▶

Start a
Program

Switch Between
Programs

**Quit the
MS-DOS Shell**

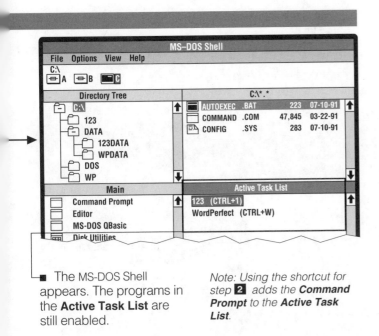

■ The MS-DOS Shell appears. The programs in the **Active Task List** are still enabled.

*Note: Using the shortcut for step 2 adds the **Command Prompt** to the **Active Task List**.*

START THE MS-DOS SHELL

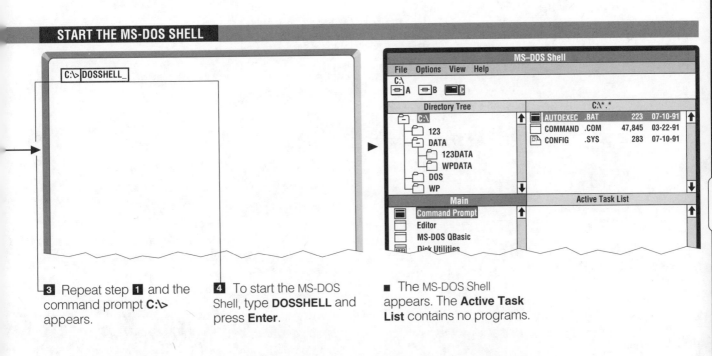

3 Repeat step 1 and the command prompt **C:\>** appears.

4 To start the MS-DOS Shell, type **DOSSHELL** and press **Enter**.

■ The MS-DOS Shell appears. The **Active Task List** contains no programs.

4. Repeat steps **1** and **2** and the command prompt **C:\>** appears.

5. To start the MS-DOS Shell, type **DOSSHELL** and press **Enter**.

• The MS-DOS Shell appears. The **Active Task List** contains no programs.

Using the
MS-DOS
Shell

Getting
Started

Managing
Your
Directories

Managing
Your
Programs

Managing
Your
Files

Disk
Utilities

CHANGE VIEWS

To help optimize file management, the MS-DOS Shell can be displayed in the Single File List or Dual File Lists view.

1 Press **Alt,V,S** to display the **Single File List** view.

or

Press **Alt,V,D** to display the **Dual File Lists** view.

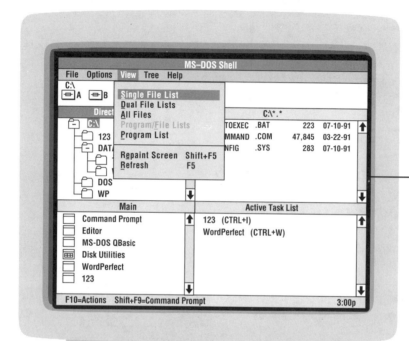

USING THE MOUSE

1. Click **View** to open its menu.

2. Click **Single File List** to view it.

or

Click **Dual File Lists** to view it.

Change
Views

Select
Multiple Files

Search for
Files

Sort
Files

Copy or Move
Files

Rename
Files

Delete
Files

SINGLE FILE LIST

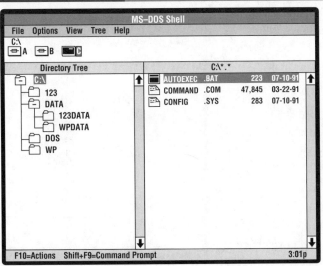

The **Single File List** view is preferred when you have a lot of directories and files and want to display them using the entire screen.

This view is also used to copy or move files between directories and drives.

DUAL FILE LISTS

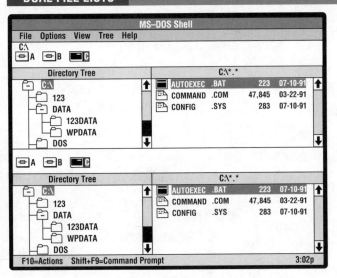

The **Dual File Lists** view is used to copy or move files between directories and drives.

Both the top and bottom areas on the screen can be changed independently to view any drive, directory and associated files in their respective areas.

Using the
MS-DOS
Shell

Getting
Started

Managing
Your
Directories

Managing
Your
Programs

Managing
Your
Files

Disk
Utilities

SELECT MULTIPLE FILES

Normally, files are created using application software (such as word processing, spreadsheet, graphic packages, etc.). The method below should only be used to create practice files.

Example: Create a file named PROJECT1.WK1 and save it to the C:\DATA\123DATA directory.

1 Press **Shift+F9** to return to the MS-DOS command prompt. If you are not in drive C:, type **C:** and press **Enter**.

2 To change the current directory to \DATA\123DATA, type **CD\DATA\123DATA** and press **Enter**.

3 Type **COPY CON PROJECT1.WK1** and press **Enter**.

4 Type any character (example: A to Z). If you want the file to contain 2 bytes, type the character twice.

5 Press **F6** or **Ctrl-Z** (hold down **Ctrl** while you press **Z**). Then press **Enter** and the file is copied to the \DATA\123DATA directory and named PROJECT1.WK1.

Example: Create a file named 1QPROFIT.MEM and save it to the C:\DATA\WPDATA directory.

1 If you are not in drive C:, type **C:** and press **Enter**.

2 To change the current directory to \DATA\WPDATA, type **CD\DATA\WPDATA** and press **Enter**.

3 Type **COPY CON 1QPROFIT.MEM** and press **Enter**.

4 Type any character (example: A to Z). If you want the file to contain 2 bytes, type the character twice.

5 Press **F6** or **Ctrl-Z** (hold down **Ctrl** while you press **Z**). Then press **Enter** and the file is copied to the \DATA\WPDATA directory and named 1QPROFIT.MEM.

---

*Note: To return to the MS-DOS Shell, type **EXIT** and press **Enter**. Then press **F5** to **Refresh** the screen.*

SELECT A GROUP OF FILES IN SEQUENCE

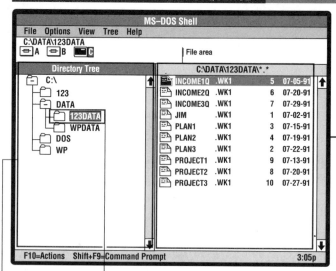

Multiple file selection is very useful for moving, copying and deleting groups of files.

1 Press **Alt,V,S** to view the **Single File List**.

2 Press **Tab** until the **Directory Tree** area is selected.

3 Press **Ctrl+*** to expand all branches.

4 To select a directory (example: **\DATA\123DATA**), press ⬇ or ⬆ until its folder is selected.

1. Click **View** to open its menu

2. Click **Single File List** to view it.

3. Press **Ctrl+*** to expand all branches.

4. Click a folder's name (example: **123DATA**) to select its directory (example: **\DATA\123DATA**).

SELECT MULTIPLE GROUP OF FILES

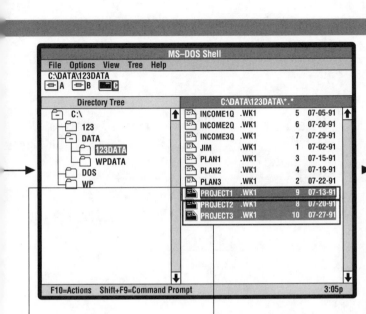

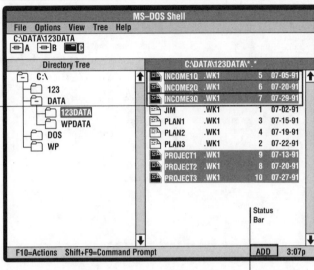

5 Press **Tab** until the **File** area is selected.

6 Press ▼ or ▲ until the first file in the group is selected (example: **PROJECT1.WK1**).

7 Hold down **Shift** and press ▼ or ▲ until the file at the end of the group is selected (example: **PROJECT3.WK1**).

TO CANCEL A SINGLE OR MULTIPLE GROUP

Press ▼ or ▲.

8 Press **Shift+F8**. The word **ADD** appears in the Status Bar.

9 Press ▲ until the first file of the second group is highlighted (example: **INCOME3Q.WK1**).

10 Press **Spacebar** to select **INCOME3Q.WK1**.

11 Hold down **Shift** and press ▲ until the file at the end of the second group is selected (example: **INCOME1Q.WK1**).

12 Press **Shift+F8** to complete the selection. **ADD** disappears from the Status Bar.

---

5. Click a file to select the first file in the group (example: **PROJECT1.WK1**).

6. To select the group, hold down **Shift** and click the file at the end of the group (example: **PROJECT3.WK1**).

TO CANCEL A SINGLE OR MULTIPLE GROUP

Click any file.

7. Hold down **Ctrl** and click the first file of the second group (example: **INCOME3Q.WK1**).

8. To select the second group, hold down **Ctrl+Shift** and click the file at the end of the second group (example: **INCOME1Q.WK1**).

Using the MS-DOS Shell

Getting Started

Managing Your Directories

Managing Your Programs

Managing Your Files

Disk Utilities

SELECT
MULTIPLE FILES

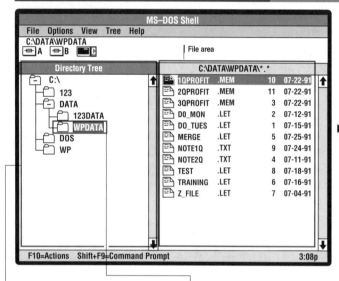

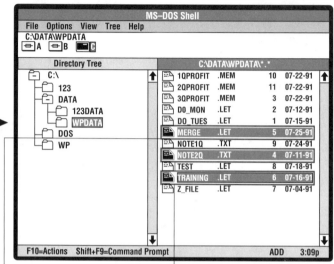

1 Press **Tab** until the **Directory Tree** area is selected.

2 To select a directory (example: **\DATA\WPDATA**), press ⬇ or ⬆ until its folder is selected.

3 Press **Tab** until the **File** area is selected.

4 Press ⬇ or ⬆ until the first file is selected (example: **MERGE.LET**).

5 Press **Spacebar** to select **MERGE.LET**.

6 Press **Shift+F8**. The word **ADD** appears in the Status Bar.

7 Press ⬇ until the second file is highlighted (example: **NOTE2Q.TXT**).

8 Press **Spacebar** to select **NOTE2Q.TXT**.

9 Press ⬇ until the third file is highlighted (example: **TRAINING.LET**).

10 Press **Spacebar** to select **TRAINING.LET**.

11 Press **Shift+F8** to complete the selection. **ADD** disappears from the Status Bar.

USING THE MOUSE

1. Click anywhere in the **Directory Tree** area to select it.

2. Click a folder (example: **WPDATA** folder) to select its directory (example: **\DATA\WPDATA**).

3. Click the first file you want to select (example: **MERGE.LET**).

4. Hold down **Ctrl** and click the other files you want to select (example: **NOTE2Q.TXT** and **TRAINING.LET**).

Change
Views

**Select
Multiple Files**

Search for
Files

Sort
Files

Copy or Move
Files

Rename
Files

Delete
Files

SELECT ALL FILES

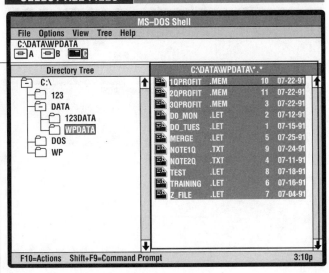

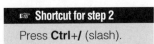

 **1** Press **Tab** until the **File** area is selected.

2 To select all files, press **Alt,F,S**.

☞ **Shortcut for step 2**

Press **Ctrl+/** (slash).

 **USING THE MOUSE**

1. Click anywhere in the **File** area to select it.

2. Click **File** to open its menu.

3. Click **Select All** to select all the files.

DESELECT ALL FILES

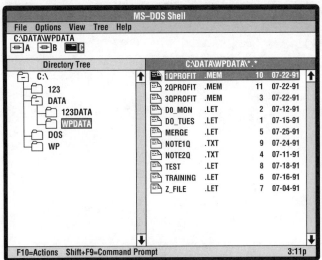

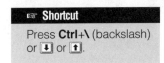

 **1** To deselect all files, press **Alt,F,L**.

☞ **Shortcut**

Press **Ctrl+** (backslash) or 🔽 or 🔼.

 **USING THE MOUSE**

1. To deselect all files, click any file.

Using the
MS–DOS
Shell

Getting
Started

Managing
Your
Directories

Managing
Your
Programs

**Managing
Your
Files**

Disk
Utilities

SEARCH FOR FILES

USING THE * WILDCARD

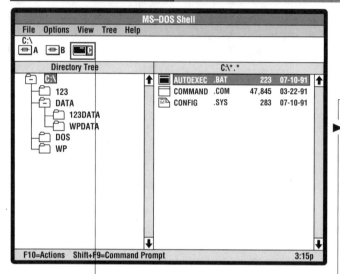

When you use an * (asterisk) in a filename or extension, the * is interpreted to mean any number of characters, from one character up to an entire filename or extension. This is useful for finding files containing groups of characters (example: BUDGET, NOTE, TRIP, WK1, etc.).

Note: Files found in the "Search Results for" screen can be moved or copied to other directories. However, files from other directories cannot be moved or copied to the "Search Results for" screen.

Files in the "Search Results for" screen can also be deleted or renamed.

Search for all files on drive C: with the extension .WK1

1 Press **Tab** until the **Disk Drive** area is selected.

2 To change to another drive (example: drive **C:**), press ← or → until drive **C:** is selected.

3 Press **Alt,F,H** to access the **Search File** dialog box.

USING THE MOUSE

1. Click drive **C:** to select it.

2. Click the **File** menu to open it.

3. Click **Search** to access its dialog box.

Change
Views

Select
Multiple Files

Search for
Files

Sort
Files

Copy or Move
Files

Rename
Files

Delete
Files

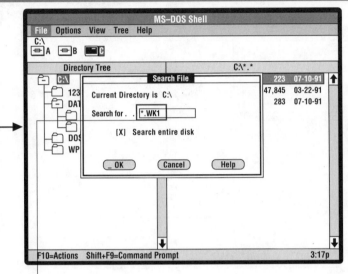

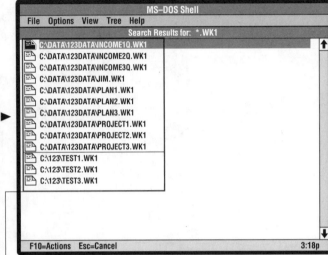

4 Type ***.WK1** in the
Search for area of the
dialog box.

*Note: If you make a mistake
typing, press **Backspace** and
then retype.*

5 Press **Enter**.

*Note: To search for a specific
file (example: PLAN1.WK1):*

– *Type **PLAN.WK1***

– *Press **Enter**.*

– *MS-DOS commands are
not case sensitive. You
can type **PLAN.WK1** or
plan.wk1.*

■ The search found **10** files
in the **C:\DATA\123DATA**
directory and **3** files in the
C:\123 directory that satisfied the search criteria.

6 Press **Esc** to reset the
screen.

4. Type ***.WK1** and click the
OK button.

*Note: If you make a mistake
typing, press **Backspace** and
then retype.*

*Note: To search for a specific
file (example: PLAN1.WK1):*

– *Type **PLAN.WK1***

– *Click the **OK** button.*

– *MS-DOS commands are
not case sensitive. You
can type **PLAN.WK1** or
plan.wk1.*

Using the
MS-DOS
Shell

Getting
Started

Managing
Your
Directories

Managing
Your
Programs

Managing
Your
Files

Disk
Utilities

SEARCH FOR FILES

USING THE ? WILDCARD

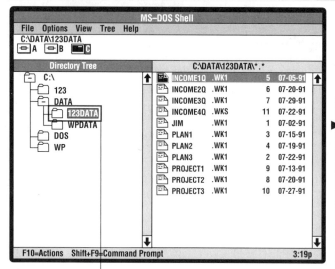

When you use a ? (question mark) in a filename or extension, the ? is interpreted to mean any character in that position. This is useful for finding files with similar names.

Note: For this example we have added a file named INCOME4Q.WKS.

Search for all files in the C:\DATA\123DATA directory whose filenames begin with INCOME and end with Q, with the extension .WK1

1 Type **Alt,T,A** to expand all branches of the **Directory Tree**.

2 Press ↓ until the **123DATA** directory is selected. The files it contains are displayed in the **File** area to the right.

3 Press **Alt,F,H** to access the **Search file** dialog box.

USING THE MOUSE

1. Click **Tree** to open its menu.

2. Click **Expand All** to open all branches of the **Directory Tree**.

3. Click the **123DATA** folder to select it.

4. Click **File** to open its menu.

5. Click **Search** to access its dialog box.

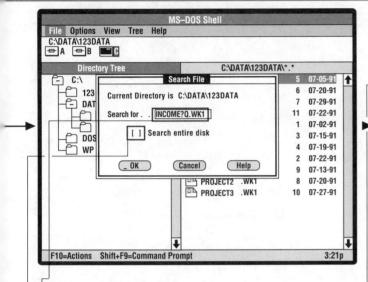

4 Type **INCOME?Q.WK1** in the **Search for** area of the dialog box.

5 Press **Tab** until the **Search entire disk** box is selected (the cursor is under the **[X]**).

6 Press **Spacebar** to turn it **off** (the **X** disappears).

Note: This speeds up the search because only the current directory 123DATA is searched.

7 Press **Enter**.

■ The search found **3** files in the **C:\DATA\123DATA** directory that satisfied the search criteria.

Note: If you had not turned off Search entire disk in step 5, files satisfying the search criteria in other directories may have been found.

INCOME4Q.WKS was not selected because of the letter S in its file extension.

8 Press **Esc** to reset the screen.

---

6. Type **INCOME?Q.WK1** in the **Search for** area of the dialog box.

7. Click the **Search entire disk** box to turn it **off** (the **X** disappears).

Note: This speeds up the search because only the current directory 123DATA is searched.

8. Click the **OK** button.

• The search found **3** files in the **C:\DATA\123DATA** directory that satisfied the search criteria.

Note: If you had not turned off Search entire disk in step 7., files satisfying the search criteria in other directories may have been found.

INCOME4Q.WKS was not selected because of the letter S in its file extension.

9. Press **Esc** to reset the screen.

Using the MS-DOS Shell

Getting Started

Managing Your Directories

Managing Your Programs

Managing Your Files

Disk Utilities

◀ 99

SORT
FILES

CHANGE THE FILE SORT DISPLAY

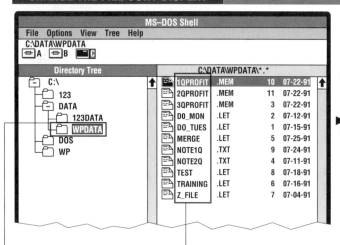

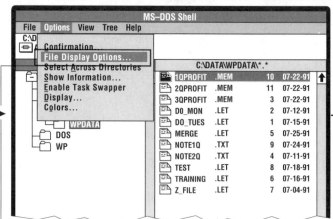

Files can be numerically and alphabetically sorted by Name, Extension, Date, Size and DiskOrder.

1 Type **Alt,T,A** to expand all the branches of the **Directory Tree**.

2 Press ⬇ until a directory is selected (example: **WPDATA** directory). The files it contains are displayed in the right area of the screen.

■ In this screen, the files are sorted numerically and alphabetically by **Name** in **ascending order**.

Note: This is because the default setting for the File Display Options dialog box (refer to the screen on page 101) is Sort by Name.

3 Press **Alt,O,F** to select **File Display Options** and display its dialog box.

USING THE MOUSE

1. Click **Tree** to open its menu.

2. Click **Expand All** to expand all branches.

3. Click any folder (example: **WPDATA** folder) to select it.

4. Click **Options** to open its menu.

5. Click **File Display Options** to access its **File Display Options** dialog box.

Change
Views

Select
Multiple Files

Search for
Files

**Sort
Files**

Copy or Move
Files

Rename
Files

Delete
Files

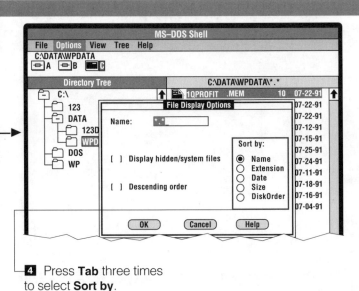

4 Press **Tab** three times to select **Sort by**.

To change your choice press ⬇ or ⬆.

DISPLAY FILES IN DESCENDING ORDER

■ Press **Tab** until the **Descending order** box is selected (the cursor is in the box [_]).

■ Press **Spacebar** to turn it **on** (an **[X]** appears).

SORT SPECIFIC FILES

■ Press **Tab** until the **Name** box is selected. If you only want to sort files with the extension .LET, type ***.LET**.

■ If you make a mistake typing, press **Backspace** and retype.

DISPLAY HIDDEN/ SYSTEM FILES

This is for advanced users. Refer to your Microsoft MS-DOS User's Guide.

6. To select **Sort by**, click ⭕ next to **Name**, **Extension**, **Date**, **Size** or **DiskOrder**.

DISPLAY FILES IN DESCENDING ORDER

■ Click the **Descending order** box to turn it **on** (an **[X]** appears).

SORT SPECIFIC FILES

■ Click in the **Name** box to select it. If you only want to sort files with .TXT extension, type ***.TXT**.

■ If you make a mistake typing, press **Backspace** and retype.

DISPLAY HIDDEN/ SYSTEM FILES

This is for advanced users. Refer to your Microsoft MS-DOS User's Guide.

Using the
MS-DOS
Shell

Getting
Started

Managing
Your
Directories

Managing
Your
Programs

Managing
Your
Files

Disk
Utilities

SORT
FILES

BY FILE EXTENSION

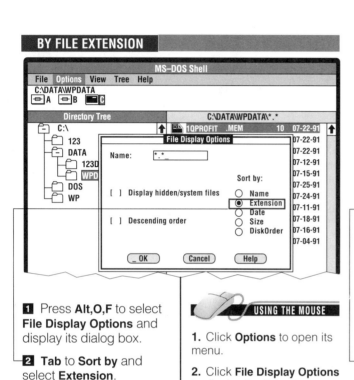

1 Press **Alt,O,F** to select **File Display Options** and display its dialog box.

2 Tab to **Sort by** and select **Extension**.

3 Press **Enter**.

USING THE MOUSE

1. Click **Options** to open its menu.

2. Click **File Display Options** to display its dialog box.

3. Click **Extension** to turn it on ⦿.

4. Click the **OK** button.

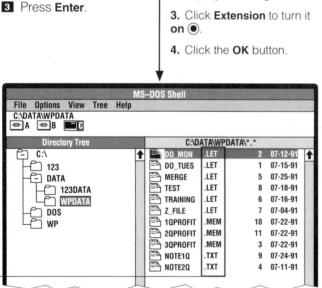

4 The files are sorted by **Extension** in alphabetical order.

BY DATE IN DESCENDING ORDER

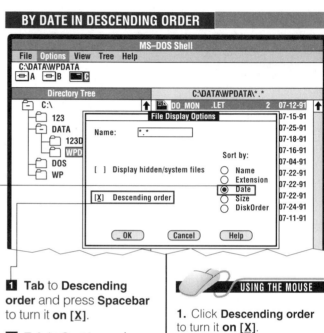

1 Tab to **Descending order** and press **Spacebar** to turn it on **[X]**.

2 Tab to **Sort by** and select **Date**.

3 Press **Enter**.

USING THE MOUSE

1. Click **Descending order** to turn it on **[X]**.

2. Click **Date** to turn it on ⦿.

3. Click the **OK** button.

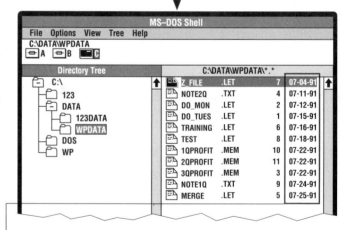

4 The files are sorted by **Date** in descending order (displaying the oldest files first).

Change
Views

Select
Multiple Files

Search for
Files

**Sort
Files**

Copy or Move
Files

Rename
Files

Delete
Files

BY SIZE (FOR ALL FILES WITH .LET EXTENSION)

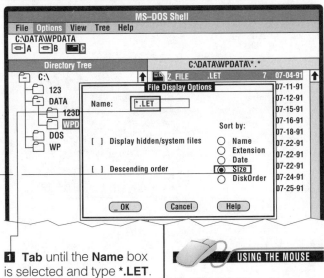

1 **Tab** until the **Name** box is selected and type ***.LET**.

2 **Tab** to **Sort by** and select **Size**.

3 Press **Enter**.

USING THE MOUSE

1. Click the **Name** box and then drag across the text to select it.

2. Type ***.LET**.

3. Click **Size** to turn it on ⦿.

4. Click the **OK** button.

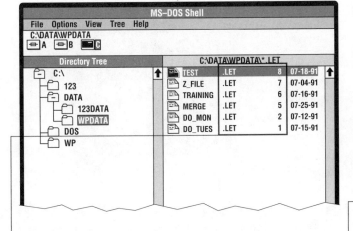

4 The **.LET** files are sorted by **Size**.

BY DISKORDER

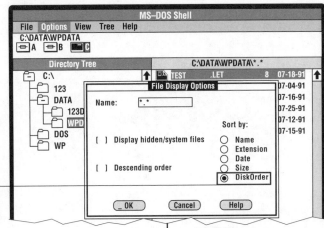

1 **Tab** to **Sort by** and select **DiskOrder**.

2 Press **Enter**.

USING THE MOUSE

1. Click **DiskOrder** to turn it on ⦿.

2. Click the **OK** button.

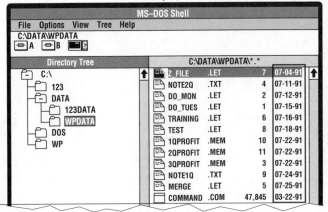

3 The files are sorted by **DiskOrder** (the order they were entered on the disk).

Note: When a file (example: COMMAND.COM is copied to a directory, it always appears at the end of the File list (regardless of the date it was created) when sorted by DiskOrder.

Using the MS-DOS Shell

Getting Started

Managing Your Directories

Managing Your Programs

Managing Your Files ◀

Disk Utilities

◀ 103

COPY OR MOVE FILES

COPY FILES TO A DIFFERENT DRIVE

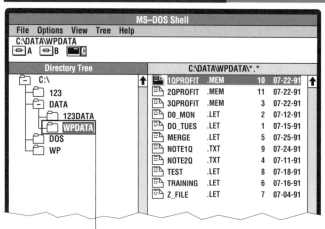

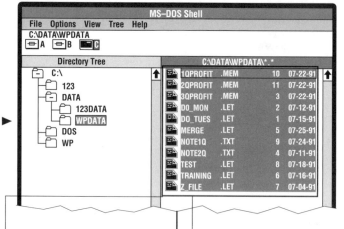

Suppose you want to copy all the files in the C:\DATA\WPDATA directory to the root directory of a floppy disk in drive A:

This is useful for backing up data files to a floppy disk.

Note: Make sure you have a formatted floppy disk in drive A:

1 Press **Tab** until the **Directory Tree** area is selected.

Note: If the DATA folder contains a (+) sign, press [↓] until the DATA folder is selected. Press * to expand its branches.

2 Press [↓] until the **WPDATA** folder is selected.

3 Press **Tab** to select the **File** area.

4 Press **Ctrl+/** to select all the files in the **C:\DATA\WPDATA** directory.

Note: To select and copy other combinations of multiple files, refer to page 92.

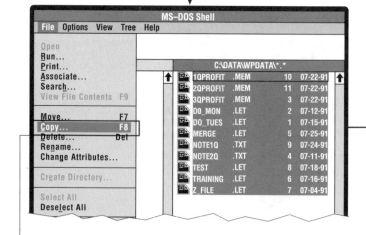

5 Press **Alt,F,C** to select the **Copy** command.

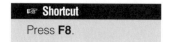

Press **F8**.

Change
Views

Select
Multiple Files

Search for
Files

Sort
Files

**Copy or Move
Files**

Rename
Files

Delete
Files

CONFIRM THE COPY

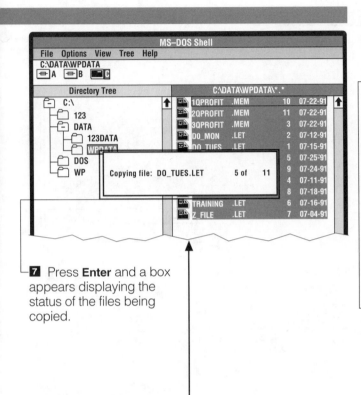

7 Press **Enter** and a box appears displaying the status of the files being copied.

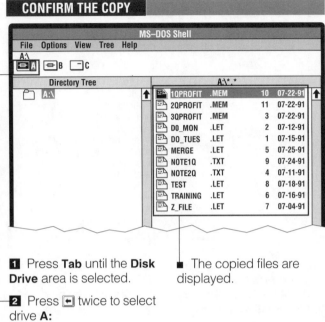

1 Press **Tab** until the **Disk Drive** area is selected.

2 Press ◄ twice to select drive **A:**

3 Press **Enter**.

■ The copied files are displayed.

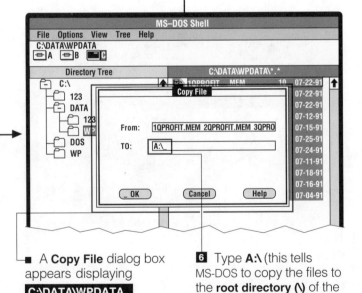

■ A **Copy File** dialog box appears displaying **C:\DATA\WPDATA_**.

6 Type **A:** (this tells MS-DOS to copy the files to the **root directory (\)** of the floppy disk in drive **A:**).

*Note: Typing **A:** overwrites* **C:\DATA\WPDATA_** .

TO MOVE FILES INSTEAD OF COPYING THEM.

The same procedure applies, except press **Alt,F,M** or **F7** in step **5** .

*Note: All the dialog boxes display **Move** instead of **Copy**.*

When a file is copied, the original file is retained.

When a file is moved, the original file is copied to a new destination and then it (the original file) is deleted.

Using the
MS-DOS
Shell

Getting
Started

Managing
Your
Directories

Managing
Your
Programs

Managing
Your
Files

Disk
Utilities

COPY OR MOVE FILES

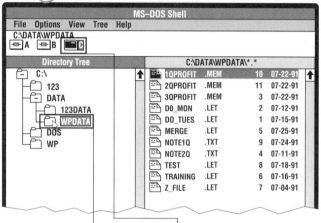

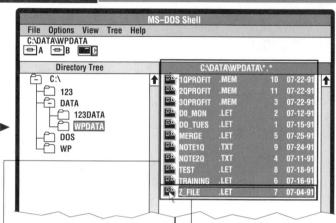

Suppose you want to copy all the files in the C:\DATA\WPDATA directory to the root directory of a floppy disk in drive A:

This is useful for backing up data files to a floppy disk.

Note: Make sure you have a formatted floppy disk in drive A:

1 Click the drive (example **C:**) which contains the files to be copied.

2 Click the **DATA** folder to open its folder.

3 Click the **WPDATA** folder to select its directory.

4 Click anywhere in the **File** area to select it.

5 Click the first file in the group to be copied (example: **1QPROFIT.MEM**).

6 To select the group, hold down **Shift** and click the last file in the group (example: **Z_FILE**).

Note: To select and copy other combinations of multiple files, refer to page 92.

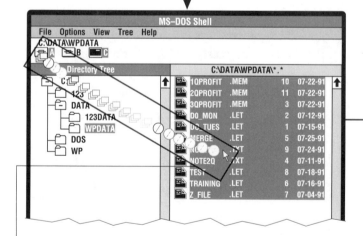

7 Position the mouse pointer ⌖ anywhere in the selected **File** area. Click and hold down the left button as you drag the mouse ⌖ over the **drive icon A**. The **A** is highlighted when it is selected.

Note: As you move the mouse, it changes from ⌖ to ⦸ to ⊡.

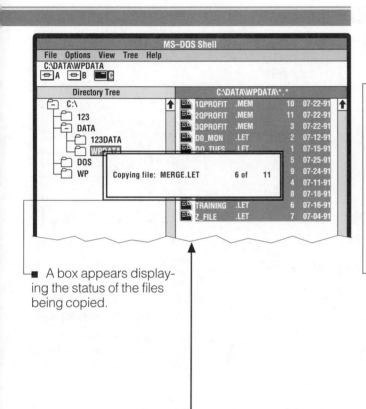

■ A box appears displaying the status of the files being copied.

CONFIRM THE COPY

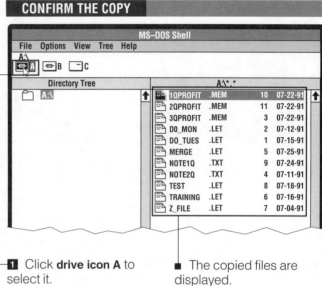

1 Click **drive icon A** to select it.

■ The copied files are displayed.

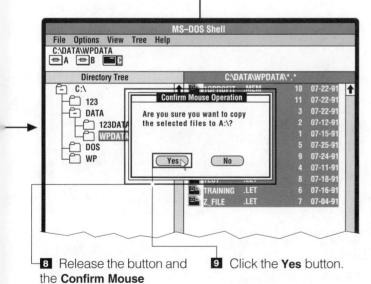

8 Release the button and the **Confirm Mouse Operation** dialog box appears.

9 Click the **Yes** button.

TO MOVE FILES INSTEAD OF COPYING THEM.

The same procedure applies, except hold down **Alt** before you begin step **7**. Release both **Alt** and the button in step **8**.

*Note: All the dialog boxes display **Move** instead of **Copy**.*

When a file is copied, the original file is retained.

When a file is moved, the original file is copied to a new destination and then it (the original file) is deleted.

Using the MS-DOS Shell

Getting Started

Managing Your Directories

Managing Your Programs

Managing Your Files

Disk Utilities

MOVE FILES FROM ONE DIRECTORY TO ANOTHER WITHIN THE SAME DRIVE

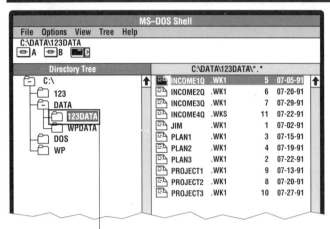

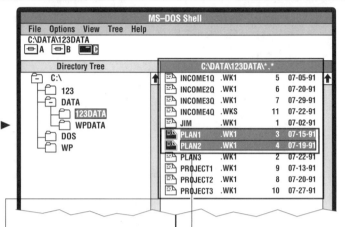

Suppose you want to move files PLAN1.WK1 and PLAN2.WK1 in the C:\DATA\123DATA directory to the C:\DATA directory.

1 Press **Tab** until the **Directory Tree** area is selected.

*Note: If the DATA folder contains a (+) sign, press ↓ until the DATA folder is selected. Press * to expand its branches.*

2 Press ↓ until the **123DATA** folder is selected.

3 Press **Tab** to select the **File** area.

4 Press ↓ until **PLAN1.WK1** is selected. Hold down **Shift** and press ↓ to select **PLAN2.WK1**.

Note: To select and copy other combinations of multiple files, refer to page 92.

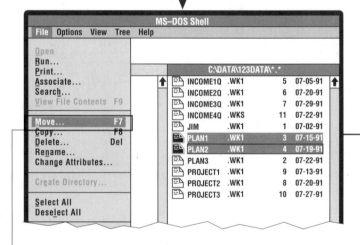

5 Press **Alt,F,M** to select the **Move** command.

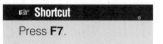

Press **F7**.

Change
Views

Select
Multiple Files

Search for
Files

Sort
Files

**Copy or Move
Files**

Rename
Files

Delete
Files

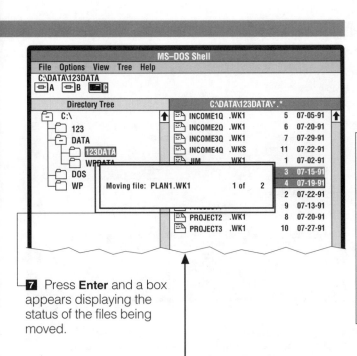

7 Press **Enter** and a box appears displaying the status of the files being moved.

■ A **Move File** dialog box appears displaying **C:\DATA\123DATA_** .

6 Type **C:\DATA** (this tells MS-DOS to move the files to the **C:\DATA** directory).

Note: Typing C:\DATA overwrites C:\DATA\123DATA_.

CONFIRM THE COPY

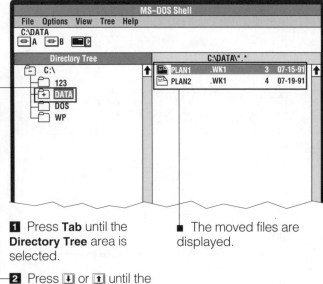

1 Press **Tab** until the **Directory Tree** area is selected.

2 Press ↓ or ↑ until the **DATA** folder is selected.

■ The moved files are displayed.

TO COPY FILES INSTEAD OF MOVING THEM.

The same procedure applies, except press **Alt,F,C** in step **5** .

*Note: All the dialog boxes display **Copy** instead of **Move**.*

When a file is copied, the original file is retained.

When a file is moved, the original file is copied to a new destination and then it (the original file) is deleted.

Using the
MS-DOS
Shell

Getting
Started

Managing
Your
Directories

Managing
Your
Programs

**Managing
Your
Files**

Disk
Utilities

COPY OR MOVE FILES

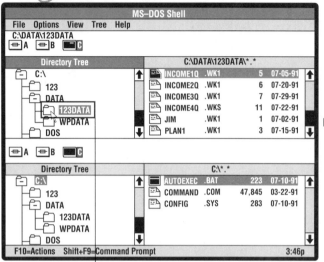

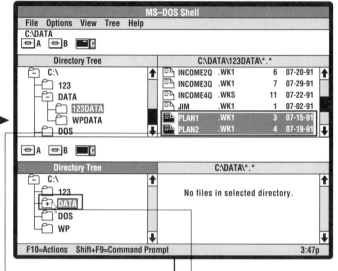

Suppose you want to move the files PLAN1.WK1 and PLAN2.WK1 in the C:\DATA\123DATA directory to the C:\DATA directory.

*Note: This example uses the **Dual File Lists** view to copy or move files. The **Single File List** view can also be used for this procedure.*

1 Click **View** to open its menu.

2 Click **Dual File Lists** to view it.

*Note: If the **DATA** folder contains a (+) sign, click it to display the **123DATA** folder.*

3 Click the **123DATA** folder in the top area of the screen to select its directory.

4 Click **PLAN1.WK1** to select it. Hold down **Shift** and click **PLAN2.WK1** to select it.

Note: To select and move other combinations of multiple files, refer to page 92.

5 Click the **DATA** folder in the lower area of the screen to select it.

Note: Its directory does not contain any files.

Change
Views

Select
Multiple Files

Search for
Files

Sort
Files

**Copy or Move
Files**

Rename
Files

Delete
Files

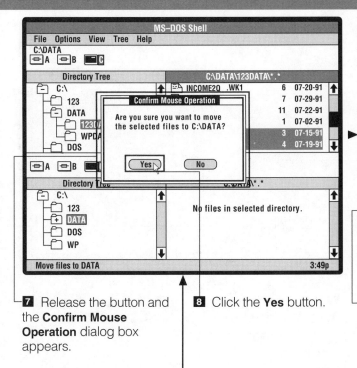

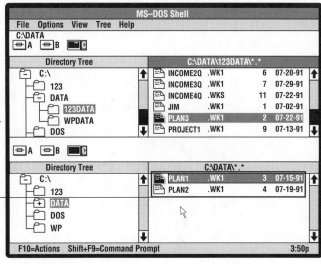

7 Release the button and the **Confirm Mouse Operation** dialog box appears.

8 Click the **Yes** button.

■ The files in the **C:\DATA\123DATA** directory are moved to the **C:\DATA** directory.

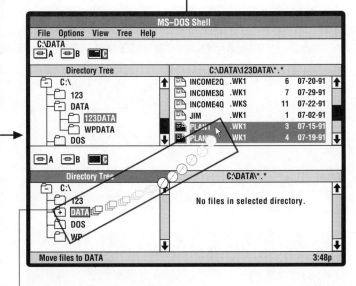

6 Move the mouse ⌖ over **PLAN1.WK1**. Click and hold down the left button, and then drag the mouse until it is over **DATA** in the lower **Directory Tree** area.

TO COPY FILES INSTEAD OF MOVING THEM.

The same procedure applies, except hold down **Ctrl** before you begin step **6**. Release both **Ctrl** and the button in step **7**.

*Note: All the dialog boxes display **Copy** instead of **Move**.*

When a file is copied, the original file is retained.

When a file is moved, the original file is copied to a new destination and then it (the original file) is deleted.

Using the
MS-DOS
Shell

Getting
Started

Managing
Your
Directories

Managing
Your
Programs

**Managing
Your
Files**

Disk
Utilities

RENAME FILES

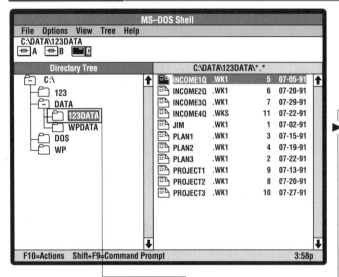

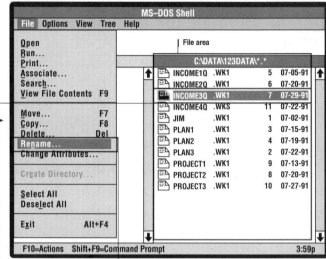

Rename the file INCOME3Q.WK1 to BUDGET3Q.WK1 in the \DATA\123DATA directory.

1 Press **Alt,V,S** to display the **Single File List** view.

2 Press **Tab** until the **Directory Tree** area is selected.

*Note: If the **DATA** folder contains a (+) sign, press ⬇ until the **DATA** folder is selected. Then press * to expand its branches.*

3 Press ⬇ until the **123DATA** folder is selected. The files in its directory are then displayed on the right side of the screen.

4 Press **Tab** until the **File** area is selected.

5 Press ⬇ until **INCOME3Q.WK1** is selected.

6 Press **Alt,F,N** to select the **Rename** command.

USING THE MOUSE

1. Click **View** to open its menu.

2. Click **Single File List** to view it.

3. Click the **123DATA** folder to select it.

4. Click **INCOME3Q.WK1** to select it.

5. Click **File** to open its menu.

6. Click **Rename** to select it.

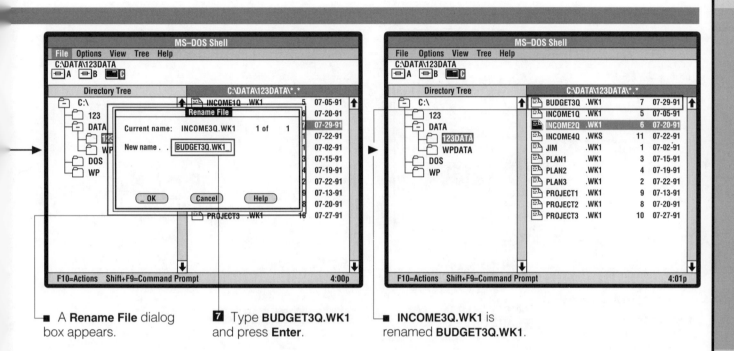

■ A **Rename File** dialog box appears.

7 Type **BUDGET3Q.WK1** and press **Enter**.

■ INCOME3Q.WK1 is renamed **BUDGET3Q.WK1**.

• The **Rename File** dialog box appears.

7. Type **BUDGET3Q.WK1**.

8. Click the **OK** button.

• INCOME3Q.WK1 is renamed **BUDGET3Q.WK1**.

Using the MS-DOS Shell

Getting Started

Managing Your Directories

Managing Your Programs

Managing Your Files

Disk Utilities

DELETE FILES

DELETE SINGLE OR MULTIPLE FILES

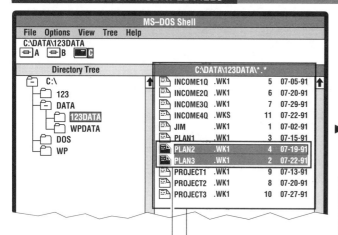

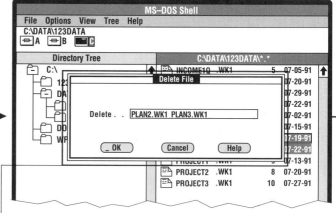

Delete files PLAN2.WK1 and PLAN3.WK1 from the \DATA\123DATA directory.

Note: You can also delete single or multiple combinations of files using this command. To select multiple files, refer to page 92.

1 Press **Tab** to select the **File** area.

2 Press ⬇ until **PLAN2.WK1** is selected. Hold down **Shift** and press ⬇ to select **PLAN3.WK1**.

3 Press **Alt,F,D** to access the **Delete File** dialog box.

☞ **Shortcut for step 3**
Press **Delete**.

4 Press **Enter** to delete **PLAN2.WK1**.

 USING THE MOUSE

1. Click **PLAN2.WK1** to select it.

2. Hold down **Shift** and click **PLAN3.WK1** to select it.

3. Click **File** to open its menu. Click **Delete** to access the **Delete File** dialog box.

4. Click the **OK** button to delete **PLAN2.WK1**.

CHECK OR CHANGE CONFIRMATION STATUS

Note: We recommend you keep all File Options on. Then each time you delete files, or use the mouse to copy or move files—a Confirmation dialog box appears.

1 To access the **Confirmation** dialog box, press **Alt,O,C**.

2 To move through the **Confirm** options, press **Tab**.

3 To toggle between **on [X]** and **off [ ]**, press **Spacebar**.

4 To save changes, press **Enter**. To cancel changes, press **Esc**. To get Help, press **Tab** until you select **Help** and then press **Enter**.

 USING THE MOUSE

1. Click **Options** to open its menu.

2. Click **Confirmation** to display its dialog box.

3. Click a **Confirm** option to turn it **off [ ]**. To turn the same option **on [X]**, click it again.

4. To save changes, click the **OK** button. To cancel changes, click the **Cancel** button. To get help, click the **Help** button.

114 ▶

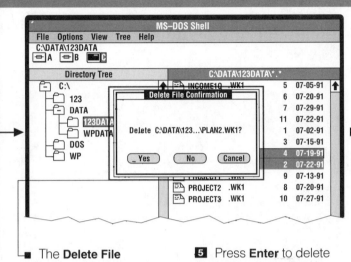

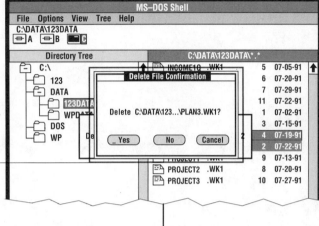

■ The **Delete File Confirmation** dialog box appears for **PLAN2.WK1**.

5 Press **Enter** to delete **PLAN2.WK1**, or press **Tab** to select the **No** button and then press **Enter**.

*Note: If you select the **No** button, MS-DOS skips to **PLAN3.WK1** without deleting **PLAN2.WK1**.*

■ The **Delete File Confirmation** dialog box appears for **PLAN3.WK1**.

6 Press **Enter** to delete **PLAN3.WK1**.

• The **Delete File Confirmation** dialog box appears for **PLAN2.WK1**.

5. Click the **Yes** button to delete **PLAN2.WK1** or click the **No** button to skip to the next file.

• The **Delete File Confirmation** dialog box appears for **PLAN3.WK1**.

6. Click the **Yes** button to delete **PLAN3.WK1**.

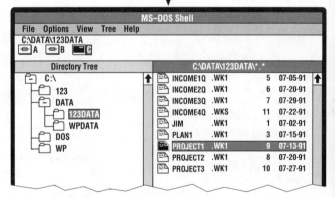

■ This screen confirms that both **PLAN2.WK1** and **PLAN3.WK1** are deleted.

Using the
MS-DOS
Shell

Getting
Started

Managing
Your
Directories

Managing
Your
Programs

**Managing
Your
Files**

Disk
Utilities

DISK COPY

DISK COPY

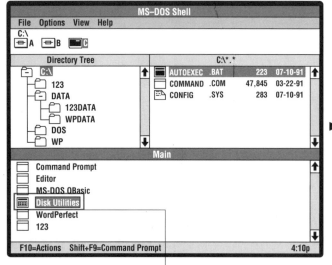

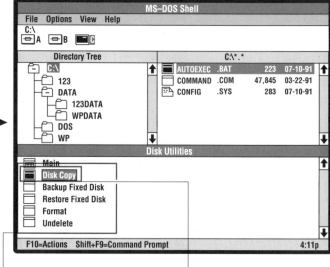

The Disk Copy command is used to copy the entire contents of one floppy disk to another, so that the second disk is an exact copy of the first.

1 Press **Alt,V,F** to display the **Program/File Lists** screen.

2 Press **Tab** until the **Main** area is selected.

3 Press ⬇ 3 times to highlight **Disk Utilities**.

4 Press **Enter** and the **Disk Utilities** appear.

5 Press ⬇ to highlight **Disk Copy**.

Caution

The Disk Copy command automatically formats the target floppy disk during the copy process, destroying its existing contents.

Make sure the target floppy disk does not contain files that you want to keep.

 USING THE MOUSE

1. Click **View** to open its menu.

2. Click **Program/File Lists** to display its view.

3. Double click **Disk Utilities**.

• The **Disk Utilities** appear.

4. Double click **Disk Copy** to select it.

116 ▶

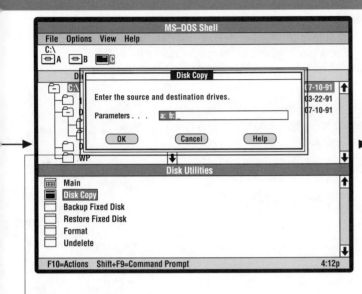

Insert SOURCE diskette in drive A:

Insert TARGET diskette in drive B:

Press any key to continue . . .

6 Press **Enter** and the **Disk Copy** dialog box appears.

DISK COPY USING TWO DRIVES

Press **Enter**.

Note: Disk Copy only works on floppy disks of the same size and capacity.

DISK COPY USING ONE DRIVE

Type **A: A:** and press **Enter**.

*Note: Make sure you leave a space between **A: A:***

7 Refer to page 52 for detailed instructions on how to **Disk Copy** using one or two floppy drives.

5. The **Disk Copy** dialog box appears.

DISK COPY USING TWO DRIVES

Click the **OK** button.

Note: Disk Copy only works on floppy disks of the same size and capacity.

DISK COPY USING ONE DRIVE

Type **A: A:** and click the **OK** button.

*Note: Make sure you leave a space between **A: A:***

6. Refer to page 52 for detailed instructions on how to **Disk Copy** using one or two floppy drives.

Using the MS-DOS Shell

Getting Started

Managing Your Directories

Managing Your Programs

Managing Your Files

Disk Utilities

BACKUP FIXED DISK

The Backup command copies data files on your hard disk to backup floppy disks. This protects your data in case of a catastrophic failure of your hard disk or accidental erasure of important files.

Backup your data files regularly (daily or weekly).

The complete Backup procedure consists of two commands—Backup and Restore. The Backup command is described on these two pages. The Restore command is described on the next two pages.

The Restore command is described on the next two pages.

BACKUP ALL FILES AND DIRECTORIES

Backup all files and directories starting from the \DATA directory to a series of floppy disks. The number of disks required depends on the total size of the files to be backed up and the size of the disks used.

Backup floppy disks required

To backup **5,500K** of data files with **720K** floppy disks requires **5,500 ÷ 720 = 8** disks.

Note: Since you already have the original application programs and MS-DOS floppy disks, these files are not normally backed up using this command.

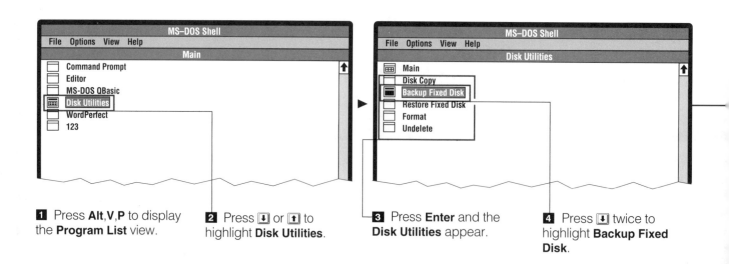

1 Press **Alt,V,P** to display the **Program List** view.

2 Press ⬇ or ⬆ to highlight **Disk Utilities**.

3 Press **Enter** and the **Disk Utilities** appear.

4 Press ⬇ twice to highlight **Backup Fixed Disk**.

USING THE MOUSE

1. Click **View** to open its menu.

2. Click **Program List** to display its view.

3. Double click **Disk Utilities**.

• The **Disk Utilities** appear.

4. Double click **Backup Fixed Disk** to select it.

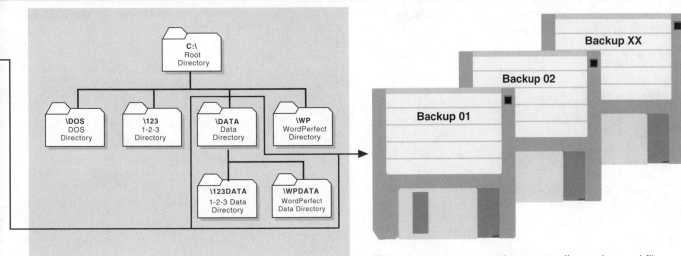

The **DATA**, **123DATA** and **WPDATA** directories and files are copied to backup floppy disks **01** to **XX**.

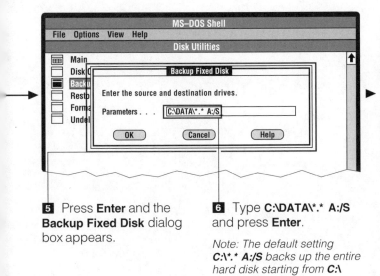

Insert backup diskette 01 in drive A:

WARNING! Files in the target drive
A:\ root directory will be erased
Press any key to continue . . .

5 Press **Enter** and the **Backup Fixed Disk** dialog box appears.

6 Type **C:\DATA*.* A:/S** and press **Enter**.

Note: The default setting C:*. A:/S backs up the entire hard disk starting from C:\ (the root directory).*

7 Refer to page 54 for detailed instructions on how to proceed from this screen.

• The **Backup Fixed Disk** dialog box appears.

5. Type **C:\DATA*.* A:/S**

6. Click the **OK** button.

7. Refer to page 54 for detailed instructions on how to proceed from this screen.

Using the
MS-DOS
Shell

Getting
Started

Managing
Your
Directories

Managing
Your
Programs

Managing
Your
Files

Disk
Utilities

RESTORE FIXED DISK

The Restore command is used to restore data files on backup floppy disks to your hard drive.

Files duplicated using the Backup command can only be accessed with the Restore command.

RESTORE ALL FILES AND DIRECTORIES

Restore all files and directories on backup floppy disks to the C:\DATA directory.

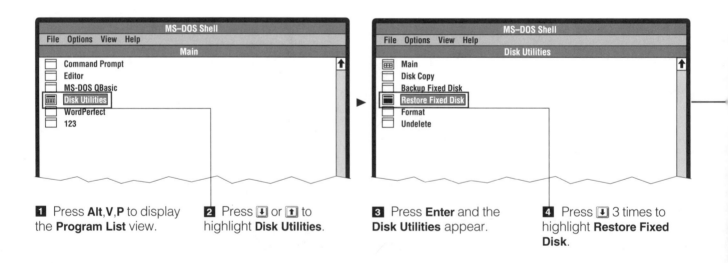

1 Press **Alt,V,P** to display the **Program List** view.

2 Press ⬇ or ⬆ to highlight **Disk Utilities**.

3 Press **Enter** and the **Disk Utilities** appear.

4 Press ⬇ 3 times to highlight **Restore Fixed Disk**.

USING THE MOUSE

1. Click **View** to open its menu.

2. Click **Program List** to display its view.

3. Double click **Disk Utilities**.

• The **Disk Utilities** appear.

4. Double click **Restore Fixed Disk** to select it.

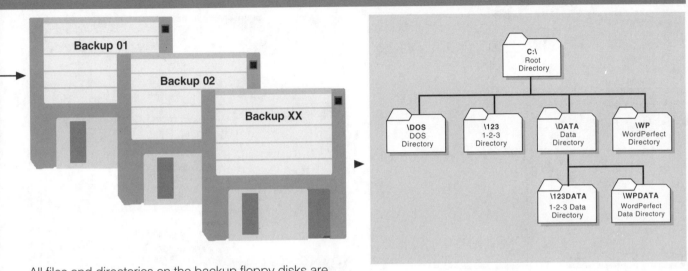

All files and directories on the backup floppy disks are copied to the **C:** hard drive **DATA**, **123DATA** and **WPDATA** directories.

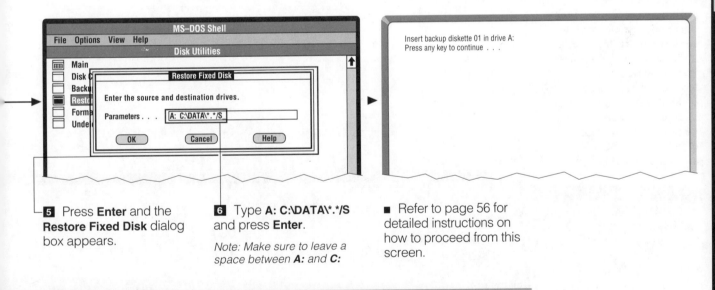

5 Press **Enter** and the **Restore Fixed Disk** dialog box appears.

6 Type **A: C:\DATA*.*/S** and press **Enter**.

*Note: Make sure to leave a space between **A:** and **C:***

■ Refer to page 56 for detailed instructions on how to proceed from this screen.

• The **Restore Fixed Disk** dialog box appears.

5. Type **A: C:\DATA*.*/S**

*Note: Make sure to leave a space between **A:** and **C:***

6. Click the **OK** button.

• Refer to page 56 for detailed instructions on how to proceed from this screen.

Using the
MS-DOS
Shell

Getting
Started

Managing
Your
Directories

Managing
Your
Programs

Managing
Your
Files

Disk
Utilities

/ FORMAT

FORMAT A FLOPPY DISK

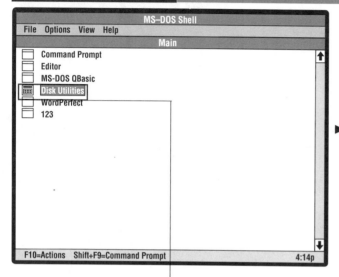

The Format command prepares a blank or previously formatted floppy disk for data and program file storage. This command checks for bad sectors on the floppy disk, and sets up a File Allocation Table (to track the location of each file on the disk). It also creates a root directory (to store the name, extension, size, creation date and time of all files on the disk).

1 Press **Alt,V,P** to display the **Program List** view.

2 Press ⬇ 3 times to highlight **Disk Utilities**.

3 Press **Enter** and the **Disk Utilities** appear.

4 Press ⬇ to highlight **Format**.

Caution

Do not format a floppy disk containing information you want to retain.

If you accidentally format a floppy disk, it may be possible to recover all the files on the disk using the Unformat command. Refer to the Microsoft User's Guide or check with a system specialist.

USING THE MOUSE

1. Click **View** to open its menu.

2. Click **Program List** to display its view.

3. Double click **Disk Utilities**.

• The **Disk Utilities** appear.

4. Double click **Format** to select it.

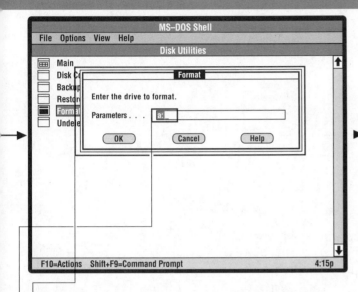

```
┌─────────────────────────────────────────┐
│              MS–DOS Shell                 │
│  File  Options  View  Help                │
│              Disk Utilities               │
│ ⊞ Main                                  ↑ │
│ ▭ Disk C┌──────────────────────────────┐ │
│ ▭ Backu │          Format              │ │
│ ▭ Restor│ Enter the drive to format.   │ │
│ ▣ Forma │                              │ │
│ ▭ Undele│ Parameters . . .  [a:_   ]   │ │
│         │                              │ │
│         │ ( OK )   ( Cancel )  ( Help ) │ │
│         └──────────────────────────────┘ │
│                                           │
│                                         ↓ │
│ F10=Actions  Shift+F9=Command Prompt 4:15p│
└───────────────────────────────────────────┘
```

```
┌───────────────────────────────────────────┐
│ Insert new diskette for drive A:            │
│ and press ENTER when ready . . .            │
│                                             │
│                                             │
└───────────────────────────────────────────┘
```

5 Press **Enter** and the **Format** dialog box appears.

6 Press **Enter** to format the floppy disk in drive **A:**

or

Type **B:** and press **Enter** to format the floppy disk in drive **B:**

Note: MS-DOS automatically formats a disk to the maximum capacity of the drive. To format a floppy disk to lower capacities, refer to F:<size> switch on page 50.

Caution

Do not format the C: drive unless you have checked with a system specialist.

■ Refer to page 48 for detailed instructions on how to proceed from this screen.

• The **Format** dialog box appears.

5. Click the **OK** button to format the floppy disk in drive **A:**

or

Type **B:** and click the **OK** button to format the floppy disk in drive **B:**

Note: MS-DOS automatically formats a disk to the maximum capacity of the drive. To format a floppy disk to lower capacities, refer to F:<size> switch on page 50.

Caution

Do not format the C: drive unless you have checked with a system specialist.

• Refer to page 48 for detailed instructions on how to proceed from this screen.

Using the
MS-DOS
Shell

Getting
Started

Managing
Your
Directories

Managing
Your
Programs

Managing
Your
Files

Disk
Utilities

UNDELETE FILES

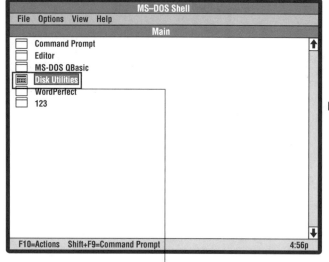

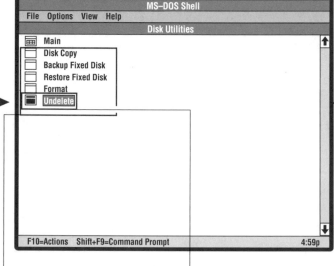

When you save a file, MS-DOS writes the file to the disk and tells a File Allocation Table (FAT) where the file is located on the disk. If a file is deleted, it still remains on the disk, but its connection to the FAT is removed.

To keep track of deleted files, a special Mirror program can be installed (refer to page 40) to detect the information required to recover deleted files.

The Undelete command restores files that were erased using the Delete command. Use the Undelete command immediately after a file is accidentally erased. Do not change or create any new files before using the Undelete command.

1 Press **Alt,V,P** to display the **Program List** view.

2 Press ⬇ or ⬆ to highlight **Disk Utilities**.

3 Press **Enter** and the **Disk Utilities** appear.

4 Press ⬇ to highlight **Undelete**.

USING THE MOUSE

1. Click **View** to open its menu.

2. Click **Program List** to display its view.

3. Double click **Disk Utilities**.

• The **Disk Utilities** appear.

4. Double click **Undelete** to select it.

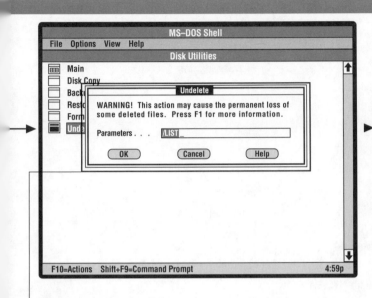

5 Press **Enter** and the
Undelete dialog box
appears.

Press Enter	To list all the deleted files.	■ Refer to page 40 for detailed instructions.
Type /ALL and press Enter	To undelete all files.	■ Refer to page 42 for detailed instructions.

Note: The files are listed or undeleted from the current directory.
If the files are in another directory, its path must be included
(example: \DATA\WPDATA/LIST or \DATA\WPDATA/ALL).

5. The **Undelete** dialog box
appears.

Click the OK button	To list all the deleted files.	• Refer to page 40 for detailed instructions.
Type /ALL and click the OK button	To undelete all files.	• Refer to page 42 for detailed instructions.

Note: The files are listed or undeleted from the current directory. If
the files are in another directory, its path must be included (ex-
ample: \DATA\WPDATA/LIST or \DATA\WPDATA/ALL).

Using the
MS-DOS
Shell

Getting
Started

Managing
Your
Directories

Managing
Your
Programs

Managing
Your
Files

Disk
Utilities

INDEX